I0412719

BLOCKADE

BLOCKADE

The Story of Jewish Immigration to Palestine
1933-1948

Gerald Ziedenberg
M.A. History

authorHOUSE®

AuthorHouse™
1663 Liberty Drive
Bloomington, IN 47403
www.authorhouse.com
Phone: 1-800-839-8640

© 2011 by Gerald Ziedenberg. All rights reserved.

No part of this book may be reproduced, stored in a retrieval system, or transmitted by any means without the written permission of the author.

First published by AuthorHouse   11/03/2011

ISBN: 978-1-4670-4405-9 (sc)
ISBN: 978-1-4670-4495-0 (hc)
ISBN: 978-1-4670-4404-2 (ebk)

Library of Congress Control Number: 2011918317

Printed in the United States of America

Any people depicted in stock imagery provided by Thinkstock are models, and such images are being used for illustrative purposes only.
Certain stock imagery © Thinkstock.

This book is printed on acid-free paper.

Because of the dynamic nature of the Internet, any web addresses or links contained in this book may have changed since publication and may no longer be valid. The views expressed in this work are solely those of the author and do not necessarily reflect the views of the publisher, and the publisher hereby disclaims any responsibility for them.

COMMENTS

"Blockade" by Gerald Ziedenberg

Finally! Mr. Ziedenberg has compiled a comprehensive historic expose of British duplicity, anti-Semitism and brutality. At a time when Nazi Germany tried to expel its Jews, Britain closed off their escape to Palestine. The British BLOCKADE unwittingly contributed to the murder of millions. The tragedy does not end there, after the end of the war the BLOCKADE prevented hundreds of thousands of Holocaust Survivors, through horrendous means, and by brutal force from reaching the Promised Land. A must read.

Nathan Leipciger, Co-president, Canadian Holocaust Survivors and Descendents.

"Many of us have visited Israel at one time or another. Yet, few of us - in particular the young ones - are aware of the heroic sacrifices many of the early immigrants had to endure, in order to enter the Holy Land, during the period of the 1930's and 1940's.

Gerald Ziedenberg, a pharmacist turned to a historian, very vividly and eloquently describes a collage of personal experiences of the early and dedicated Zionists, who dared to challenge the British soldiers and the murderous Arab tribes, who tried to stop the courageous immigrants to enter the Land of the Bible.

Yet, the large number of dedicated Zionists prevailed and eventually established the modern State of Israel.

Once one starts reading this fascinating and informative book, it is difficult to put it down. One becomes immersed in the many amazing personal stories and unbelievable challenges the early immigrants had to cope with to succeed. This book should be read by everyone, Jews and Christians alike."

"Leslie Dan, a survivor of the Holocaust"

I thought your book was excellent. It's a wonderful tribute to the men and women who suffered through this terrible ordeal, and it's so fortunate that they are still around to tell their stories. I learned so much while reading it. Books like this—labours of love that tell important stories that might otherwise be lost—are the reason I took up this profession. Despite the numerous works I've read about WWII, I never got the chance to read about the British blockade in such detail. It was truly eye opening, and a sobering reminder that the atrocities of the war were not as cut-and-dried as the winners would like us to imagine. I think it's going to be a fantastic addition to the genre of Jewish history. I think the Jewish community and the Jewish community of Toronto (my town, as well, incidentally) will eagerly embrace it.

Editor

To my grandchildren Madison, Aaron, Gabriel, and Sari, so they will
know the story of how brave people were able to found the State of Israel.

To those heroic people who participated in
this epic struggle.

ACKNOWLEDGEMENTS

To the typist, Annmarie Uleryk.

To my wife, Sheila, without whom nothing is possible.

To the numerous professors of history at the University of Toronto for their support, encouragement, and advice.

To the many interviewees listed at the end.

To the archivists at Leo Baeck Institute, Ontario Jewish Archives, the United States Holocaust Museum, and YIVO.

CONTENTS

LIST OF MAPS AND PHOTOS

Maps

Photos

CHRONOLOGY

70 CE	Destruction of second Jewish Temple
135 CE	Bar Kochba revolt crushed by the Romans
August 1897	Theodore Herzl First Zionist Congress Basel Switzerland
November 1917	Balfour Declaration
December 1917	General Allenby enters Jerusalem
1922	San Remo Conference Ratifies British Mandate
1923	Jabotinsky and Revisionists split from the Main Zionist Movement
1924	Johnson-Reed Act restricts immigration to the United States
January 30, 1933	Adolf Hitler becomes Chancellor of Germany
1935	Nuremberg Laws in Germany
1936-1938	Arab Revolt in Palestine
November 1938	Kristallnacht
1938/1939	British White Papers Restricting Jewish Immigration to Palestine
September 1, 1939	WWII begins
	Germany invades Poland
June 22, 1941	Germany invades Russia
	The mass killings of the Holocaust begin
January 20, 1942	Wannsee Conference to formulate final plans to kill 11 million Jews
May 7, 1945	World War II ends
July 1946	Kielce Pogrom. A final incentive for the remnants of Polish Jewry to leave

Summer 1945- Spring 1948	Bricha Movement to rescue the Shir Ha Pelit (the surviving remnants) to British Mandate Palestine
July 1946	King David Hotel Explosion
May 7, 1948	David Ben Gurion declares the Jewish State of Israel under a large portrait of Theodore Herzl

INTRODUCTION

On January 30, 1933, Adolf Hitler became the Chancellor of Germany. Hitler had a *weltsthung*, or worldview, that encompassed three salient points: "the extermination of the Jewish people," the destruction of what he termed Judeo-Bolshevism, and the creation of *lebensraum*, or living room, to the east. These three ideas were intertwined and led to the eventual murder of millions of Jewish people.

On December 1917, General Edmund Allenby led the British army into Jerusalem. The defeat of the Ottoman Empire in what was then Palestine by the British and the issuance of the Balfour declaration of November 2, 1917, led many Jews to aspire to a Jewish homeland in Palestine. There had been a continuous Jewish presence for two thousand years in Palestine, even after the defeat at the hands of the Romans in the Bar Kochba revolt of 135 CE. To many, Theodore Herzl, who had convened the first Zionist congress in Basel, Switzerland, in 1897, seemed to be the spark of modern Zionism. Yet in modern Zionism there had been many precursors to Herzl, people like Moses Hess and Leo Pinsker. Fierce anti-Semitism had pervaded the Tsar's Russian Empire and drove many Jews to seek refuge in Palestine. Following World War I, the Russian Revolution, and the Balfour Declaration there seemed to be a coalescing of a desire by many Jews, but certainly not a majority, to establish a Jewish homeland in the territory known as Palestine.

In 1922 at San Remo, Italy, the British administration of Palestine was formalised as an official mandate by the League of Nations. During the remaining years of the 1920s, the British maintained their presence in Palestine. Justification for the continued presence of the British in Palestine was connected by many to the Balfour Declaration. The Jewish population in Palestine slowly rose during this period as intermittent immigration continued to Palestine, mainly from Eastern Europe.

In 1928, Adolf Hitler had received only 2.8 percent of the popular vote, but by the early 1930s Adolf Hitler and his Nazi party had become a political force in Germany. Jewish unease grew not only in Germany but in many surrounding European countries as well. By the 1930s, immigration to North America, Australia, and other places of refuge was severely restricted. In December 1932, just before the Nazis came to power, Albert Einstein, the world famous Nobel Laureate, left Germany to immigrate to America. In 1933, Otto Frank left Germany to seek a new life in Amsterdam, Holland. The ascension to power of Adolf Hitler motivated more than twenty-five past and future Nobel Prize winners to leave Nazi Germany, most of them of Jewish origins. For the lucky few the opportunity to immigrate to the new world was a godsend. But for most there was no such opportunity. There was only one place that was still open to immigration: Palestine. In particular for the Jews of Germany in the early 1930s, Palestine was still an attainable destination. Those Jews who came from Eastern Europe for the most part had no such opportunity. Many had neither the money nor the connections required to immigrate to Palestine. The Jews of Soviet Russia were locked in a vast prison camp.

The Intentionalist-Functionalist Debate

The intentionalist-functionalist debate is a long-standing and perplexing argument between two opposite camps of Holocaust scholars. It is not about Holocaust denial but rather whether Adolf Hitler and his Nazi cohorts sought to destroy the Jewish race from the beginning of their rise to power or whether the Nazi extermination policies evolved as a matter of course. This debate is a key element in appreciating the failure of British Mandate authorities to allow Jews into Palestine. If, as many scholars believe, the Nazi policies evolved over time and in reaction to the policies of the Western Allies, then perhaps the admission of Jews to Palestine might have saved millions of lives.

In his 1923 book, *Mein Kampf* (*My Struggle*), Hitler wrote about gassing Jews and made several comments about Jews as vermin. From this many conclude that the Nazi extermination policies were ordained from the beginning. The evidence for the Intentionalist side tends to be based on Nazi rhetoric. Warnings and speeches are not firm foundations for the facts.

In contrast, Nazi behaviour seems to indicate the opposite. Once the Nazis came to power in 1933, every policy seemed to focus on simply getting rid of the Jews, not murdering them. The eliminationist Jewish policies appear to have started only after the Nazi conquest of Poland in September 1939.

On August 7, 1933, barely six months after Chancellor Hitler had assumed power, leaders of the Zionist movement concluded a controversial pact with the Third Reich. The so-called transfer agreement sent some 60,000 German Jews and $100 million to the Yishuv in British Mandate Palestine in return for the cessation of the worldwide Jewish boycott against Nazi Germany. The willingness of the Nazi authorities to allow German Jews to escape death seems to endorse the functionalist aspect of the Nazi aims. While it is hard to get a firm estimate, more than 100,000 Jews of German, Austrian, and Czech descent were able to escape to British Mandate Palestine. These people were able to immigrate to Palestine because the British authorities allowed their entry and the Nazis in Germany, Austria, and Czechoslovakia allowed them out. Once the Arab revolt started in 1936, the restrictions on legal immigration to the Mandate began and Jewish immigration became illegal and clandestine. Until September 1, 1939, and the beginning of the war, it is quite clear that Jews were allowed by the Nazi authorities to freely immigrate if there was somewhere for them to go.

Once Poland was conquered and the Germans had control of over 3,000,000 additional Jews, Nazi policies began to evolve. The Nazis began to cast a wide search for a place to put the millions of Jews. When France fell in 1940, thoughts were advanced about Madagascar (a French colonial possession) as a site for Jews. Other similar ideas were cancelled as the Germans did not have the shipping resources or the ability to transfer the millions of Jews under their control. It now became evident that the only way to deal with the Jews was simply to kill them. After all, no one wanted them or would let them into their countries. Beginning on June 22, 1941, with the invasion of the Soviet Union in Operation Barbarossa, mass killings of Jews began for the first time. It was only because the Jews were denied entry and access to other places that the Germans decided on their genocidal policies that became known as the Holocaust.

This is the story of Jewish immigration to Palestine—from the rise of Adolf Hitler to the creation of the State of Israel. Using numerous personal interviews, memoirs, testimonies, and archival material, a heroic saga of the mostly illegal immigration to British Mandate Palestine will be told.

CHAPTER 1

The Balfour Declaration and the British Mandate

Foreign Office,
November 2nd, 1917.

Dear Lord Rothschild,

I have much pleasure in conveying to you, on behalf of His Majesty's Government, the following declaration of sympathy with Jewish Zionist aspirations which has been submitted to, and approved by, the Cabinet:

> *"His Majesty's Government view with favour the establishment in Palestine of a national home for the Jewish people, and will use their best endeavours to facilitate the achievement of this object, it being clearly understood that nothing shall be done which may prejudice the civil and religious rights of existing non-Jewish communities in Palestine, or the rights and political status enjoyed by Jews in any other country."*

I should be grateful if you would bring this declaration to the knowledge of the Zionist Federation.

Yours sincerely,

Arthur James Balfour

Lord Balfour

On November 2, 1917, a cold drizzly day in London, England, a front-page advertisement appeared in *The Times* of London. This document, which became known as the Balfour Declaration, was an appeal to the Jewish people made by the British Foreign Secretary Lord Balfour and other members of His Majesty's Government. It was in the form of a letter to Lord Rothschild, the preeminent leader of the British Jewish community. This was the height of World War I. Millions of British and French soldiers had already been killed, and *The Times* of London was filled with casualty lists and terrible accounts of the war. The Western allies were very hard pressed and in addition anxious about their Eastern ally, the Russian Empire.

In March 1917, moderate Russian socialists led by Alexander Kerensky had overthrown the court of the Romanovs. Kerensky made a fatal error in deciding to continue prosecution of the war and refused to make any meaningful land reforms. The mammoth Russian army slowly began to fall apart, as mass desertions and mutinies took place. Then the Germans sent Vladimir Ilyich Lenin via a sealed train from Switzerland to Finland to further agitate the situation. The Germans hoped that a further insurrection would topple the moderate Russian government and force it out of the war. Above all, the Germans wanted to avoid continuing to fight a two-front war, the French and British on the western front and Russia on the eastern front.

Britain knew that Russia in the fall of 1917 was in deep trouble. The Balfour Declaration was issued for several reasons, many of them connected to the war on the eastern front. Firstly, it was felt that the Jews had a profound influence on Russian affairs. After all some 25 percent of the upper Bolshevik leadership at that time was Jewish. British theorists reasoned that the Balfour Declaration would induce Russian Jewry to help the western allied cause. Secondly, there was a strong belief by Christian fundamentalists, including David Lloyd George, that the establishment of a Jewish homeland in Palestine would herald the second coming of Christ. Thirdly, many sympathized with the Jewish people on purely humanitarian grounds and felt that a Jewish Homeland would be a good way to solve the problems of the Jewish people. Fourthly, there was a belief by many that there really was a powerful worldwide Jewish cabal that worked behind the scenes of power pulling the strings. To them, the "Protocols of Zion" was no pipedream. If these secret Jewish conspirators could be persuaded to help the British war effort, the western allies might eventually prevail. Lastly, Chaim Weizman, the great Zionist leader, had tremendously helped the British war effort with his chemical wizardry. Weizman, a world-class chemist, had developed a process involving acetone that had a profound effect on British munitions capabilities. Perhaps the British Government felt that Weizman's efforts needed to be rewarded. Whether it was one specific reason or a combination of factors, the Balfour Declaration was issued on November 2, 1917.

General Edmund Allenby had conquered the Ottoman Empire's territories in Palestine in 1917. Following Allenby's triumphal entry into Jerusalem in December 1917, the British army soon occupied most of what is now Israel. Following the end of World War I and establishment of the League of Nations, the British Mandate was established. It should be emphasized that it never dealt with geographical borders. The Mandate was further delineated at San Remo, Italy, in April 1922. The British had laid the ground for almost a century of incessant warfare when they made two very conflicting promises. Hussein ben Ali Sharif of Mecca had been promised by T. E. Lawrence (Lawrence of Arabia) most of the Arab Middle East in exchange for his support. Similarly, for the many reasons previously mentioned, the Jewish people had also been promised an opportunity for a national home. The bloodshed and acrimony started by these divergent promises may never be resolved.

Following the consolidation and approval of their mandate, the British colonial authorities soon began to organize their administration. It was very British—tea parties, cigars, gin and tonics, and all the trappings of an English colonial administration. The British in Palestine upheld the class stratified society that they brought from England and other colonial administrations. In his book, *One Palestine Complete*, historian Tom Segev described men and women sipping lemonade on terraces. The men wore pith helmets and the women shaded themselves from the sun with parasols. The upper classes of the administration went to lectures, concerts, and dances. Segev noted that the British viewed Palestine more as an emotion than a reality.

In standing by the Zionist movement at that moment in time, the British administration felt that it was gaining the support of an important and influential ally—the Jewish People.

In the first decade following the Balfour Declaration, the British Colonial Administration helped the Jews settle Palestine. The Yishuv, as it was called, soon amounted to a quasi-state. For the first decade after World War I, mass immigration of Jews was allowed and Jews were permitted to purchase land from the indigenous Arab population. The Jewish immigrants built many collective settlements and established industries and banks. The *Palestine Post*, the precursor to the English language *Jerusalem Post*, was first published in Jerusalem on December 1, 1932. The entire infrastructure for the state that was to eventually come was established in the British Mandate period.

Arab residents saw the developments in the postwar years differently. They felt that there were only two possible outcomes, either the Arabs would defeat the Zionists or the Zionists would defeat the Arabs. Britain was perpetually caught in the middle of this dilemma.

Most in the British administration identified with the Arabs, but a few were sympathetic to the Jews. One British officer is quoted by Segev as saying, "Arabs, Jews, and Christians in Syria and in Palestine they are all alike, a beastly people." There was clearly a huge disconnect between the British and their subjects. It should be borne in mind that there was a much larger percentage of Christian than Moslem Arabs residing in what was then Palestine.

Mark Twain had described Palestine in 1867 "as a desolate country whose soil is rich enough but mainly given over to weeds." He concluded that it was "a silent mournful expanse—a veritable desolation." That description changed as the Jews in Palestine began to build a future country, while the Arabs and their internecine fighting and squabbling did not react to the Jewish progress. Soon, mainly due to Jewish hard work and dedicated pioneers, the country was electrified, aquifers were built, and marshes were drained. The malaria that had plagued the early settlers was soon gone.

Even at the beginning of the British Mandate in 1917 about half the population of Jerusalem was already Jewish and had been since the middle of the nineteenth century. The Jerusalem of the early British Mandate was not the city of biblical legend. It was not the Jerusalem of Gold as sung by Naomi Shemer. Cholera and other diseases abounded. It was corrupt, backward, and filthy. For the Ottoman Empire that had ruled Jerusalem until 1917, it was not a jewel in their imperial crown. Most Jewish residents of Jerusalem prior to the British Mandate lived on donations from Jewish communities in Europe and North America.

Huge battles ensued between the British and the Jews about the use of Hebrew language. Theodore Herzl had originally wanted German to be the official language of the new Jewish state. Others had proscribed either Yiddish or English. Luckily for the Jewish people in Palestine, Hebrew prevailed. Asher Ginsberg, known as Ahad Ham, became the main supporter of Hebrew as the language of a future state. The resurrection of biblical Hebrew as a modern language became a key factor in the establishment of a new state. After the establishment of the Jewish state, the Hebrew language enabled immigrants from over a hundred different countries to integrate themselves into their new home.

Until the so-called Nebi Musa riots of 1920 there had been little overt violence between Arabs and Jews in Palestine. [1] Jewish authorities had warned the British administration that there would be major disturbances. As usual, the British authorities under reacted. Ronald Storrs, the chief British official, should have learned a lesson from the Ottoman Turks, who had heavily guarded the annual procession. The rioting that followed the procession resulted in five Jews and for Arabs being killed. Compared to the Hebron riots of 1929 and the great Arab revolt of 1936-1938, the casualties were small, but they were an ominous portent.

Following the violence of Nebi Musa, sporadic disturbances continued in British Mandate Palestine. It was clear that the continuing Jewish immigration was an anathema to the Arab population of Palestine. Not only did more than 100,000 Jews immigrate to Palestine during

---

[1]   A Moslem religious procession commemorating Moses.

the 1920s, but the Jewish immigrants also positioned themselves above most of the Arab residents in Palestinian society. They took the better jobs; they purchased large pieces of land and generally superseded the Arabs in whatever positions they had in society. Natural jealously ensued, exacerbating Arab fears and paranoia about the Jews.

The Jewish labour association called Histadrut began to run Union affairs, discriminating against Arab workers. The Jews practised socialism, a foreign concept to the Arabs. In addition, many devout Moslems were scandalized by the scanty dress of Jewish women. The Jews drank wine, another taboo to the Moslem faith. At least both sides agreed on the prohibition of pork. The culture clash was deeply felt by both parties. In addition, the Jews looked down on the Arabs, demeaning them and relegating them to inferior positions. The acrimony revolved around Jews taking over and casting the Arabs to the bottom of society. Above all, the paranoia focused on religious affairs. Any interaction between Jews and Arabs that touched religious artefacts and sites was ultimately bound to result in a conflagration.

On September 23, 1928, a dispute arose between the Moslem religious court (the Mahkameh) and the Jewish worshipers at the Western Wall (Wailing Wall). It was Kol Nidre, the eve of Yom Kippur, the Jewish Day of Atonement. A Mihitza (screen) had been set up at the wall to divide male and female Jewish worshipers—a common Jewish practise among Orthodox and some Conservative Jews. The screen, as described by British authorities, was an ordinary household item, the kind one would use to divide a bedroom. It was collapsible, a few wooden frames covered with cloth. This simple screen was to become the focal point for bloody rioting that ultimately claimed hundreds of lives.

In a typical Jewish manner, the Moslem authorities learned of the screen because of an argument between the Sephardic and Ashkenazim religious sextons (beadles or Shamuses). The Moslem religious trust, the Waqf, demanded that the screen be taken down. The Western Wall adjoins the Al-Aqska Mosque, perhaps the third most important Moslem religious site in the world next to Mecca and Medina. The Ashkenazic beadle (sexton) Noah Glasstien asked that the screen be allowed to remain until after the Yom Kippur prayers would be complete. The British authorities sensed that there would be trouble.

The Arabs predicted that this temporary screen would gradually evolve into a permanent structure. They saw this as an infringement of their religious rights and a desecration of their holy sites. Ultimately, British soldiers dragged one of the Hassidic worshipers out through the Dung gate and flung him and his screen into the nearby Kidron Valley.

The Jews had worshipped at the Western Wall since medieval times. In particular during the Ottoman Empire, Jewish worship was well tolerated. Sometimes the proverbial greasing of the palm had eased Jewish worshippers' access. Jews had been blowing the Shofar (the ram's horn) and utilizing a Torah ark, as well as using benches for many years. It was also noted that the screens had been utilized many times before. Nevertheless, this singular event involving a simple household screen set off an unstoppable chain reaction of bloody events. The many deaths that ensued have to be viewed in the larger context of the Arab fears of Jewish economic domination and interference with the Moslem religion.

In the early morning of Friday, August 23, 1929, many thousands of Arab villagers began to gather and make their way to Jerusalem. Although they were armed only with knives, sticks, and iron bars, they were going to worship at the Temple Mount. The Temple Mount, or Noble Sanctuary, signifies the Arab holy places above and adjacent to the Western or Wailing Wall. British authorities questioned the Arabs about their weapons. The reply was that the Arab villagers were concerned about Jewish attacks and provocations. After one of the Arab preachers made a fiery speech calling on the Islamic faithful to kill the Jews until their last drop of blood was spilt, the die was cast. The worshippers became an angry mob. Violence soon spread through all of Jerusalem. The Palestinian police, consisting mostly of Arabs intermixed with a few Jews and led by 175 British officers, were completely ineffectual. Soon the rioting spread to Hebron, and the bloody massacre that followed became emblazoned on Palestinian history. The preceding violence in Jerusalem had taken the lives of eight Jews and five Arabs. Unfortunately the murders in Hebron took a far larger toll. In all, sixty-seven Jews had been murdered; many of them were mutilated.

While the attack on Jews in Hebron was motivated by both fear and hatred, there were many other reasons, some of it simple looting, some for fear of economic competition, others for the cultural clashes mentioned and still others for wanton murder. It could be argued that this was not a "classic" Eastern European pogrom. The British Mandate police did try and intervene and save Jewish people. Many Arabs in the community saved Hebron's Jews wherever possible. In fact, it is remarkable that perhaps two thirds of Hebron's Jews were saved by their Arab neighbours. Nevertheless the Hebron Massacre remains until this very day a terrible blot on the record of Arab-Jewish relations in Palestine.

In the wake of the Hebron murders the future Nobel Laureate S. Y. Agnon wandered Jerusalem trying to save his many manuscripts. It was then that Agnon decided that his attitude towards the Arabs had changed. He felt the Jews must insulate themselves from the Arabs or else they would all be lost.

In 1928, an upstart and fiery demagogic German politician began to gather together his party, the Natural Socialist Democratic Workers Party (the Nazi Party) for elections in Germany. That year, Adolf Hitler and the Nazi Party gained only 2.8 percent of the popular vote. In 1930, that percentage rose to some 18 percent of the vote. By 1931 and 1932, Hitler's Nazi party was achieving close to one third of the popular vote. In December 1932, Albert Einstein left Germany never to return. On January 30, 1933, Adolf Hitler became the chancellor of Germany. The Jewish people's worst fears were now realized.

A major event reported on the front page of the January 31, 1933, edition of the *Palestine Post* was the appointment of Herr Hitler as the new German Chancellor. At this point there was no mention of Hitler's anti-Jewish policies. Only a few months later on, April 10, 1933, the *Palestine Post* reported that Jews were barred from German medical schools. This same edition reported that Dr. Chaim Weizman held numerous meetings with Arab leaders from Trans Jordan. The sheikhs expressed the strong view that they would be able to cooperate with the Jews in Palestine. Unfortunately their wishes never came true.

The *Palestine Post* reported in its editions for October 29 and 30, 1933, serious Arab violence and strikes. Many lives were reported lost in Jaffa, Haifa, and Nablus. The following day, the paper reported that the violence shifted to the holy city of Jerusalem, where several people were killed and seventeen injured. At the same time only eight months after Adolf Hitler took power a conference was convened in London for the relief of German-Jewish refugees. Hundreds of thousands of pounds sterling were collected by forty-five different organizations to help the refugees. This shows clearly how early in Hitler's regime the German Jews were threatened.

On Monday, October 28, 1935, the *Palestine Post* reported that the Nuremberg laws had been promulgated in Nazi Germany. Amidst the report it was stated that German Jews could not participate in municipal affairs, although they had to pay municipal taxes. It was also stated that Jewish blood could be used in blood transfusions without fear of racial defilement. Clearly the Jews of Palestine were well aware of the continual debasement and threats to their coreligionists in Germany.

The fate of Germany Jewry continued to occupy the attention of Palestinian Jewry. It was reported that Sir Herbert Samuel, the first high commissioner of British Mandate Palestine, launched an urgent financial appeal in America to raise funds for the beleaguered German Jews. At the same time, in January 1936, it was announced by the residing high commissioner of British Mandate Palestine that restrictions would begin to stop land sales from Arabs to Jews and that consideration would be given to stopping Jewish immigration. Clearly the British government was gradually acceding to Arab pressures.

German Jews were extremely patriotic and quite assimilated. Despite this it was clear to almost all but the very naïve that they could not continue in Hitler's Germany. There was literally nowhere for German, and after 1938 Austrian Jews, to go except Palestine. In the 1930s, prior to British restrictions, some 165,000 German Jews immigrated to Palestine. These non-Zionist Jews who were seeking a refuge became known in the Yishuv as Yekes.

The Yekes became known for their punctuality, organization, and strict adherence to all rules and regulations. The story is told of one Yeke who bought the only ticket available on the train from Haifa to Jerusalem. It was a standing-room ticket. As the train lurched along shaking from side to side, the Yeke was urged to sit down, as there were many empty seats. The Yeke refused to sit, as he had purchased only a standing room seat. The story epitomizes the Yeke's complete compliance with all rules and regulations. The Yekes, because of their superior intellect and organization, came to dominate the Israeli banking industry. In later years, these banking personnel drove many people, especially North Americans, crazy with their intensely legalistic interpretations of banking regulations.

Whether they were German Jews or other European Jews fleeing Hitler's maniacal intentions, the new immigrants soon began to threaten the Arab presence in Palestine. The Palestinian Arabs felt that they were going to be swamped. In November 1935, Muhammed Iz-al-Din-al Qassam began a guerrilla war against the British. Soon al-Qassam also began to attack Zionist targets. His followers equipped themselves with guns and bombs and established themselves at a base in the mountains. Many Arab notables despaired of their future in Palestine. They were further shaken by the large influx of Jewish immigrants. Qassam fled further into the mountains, where he eventually was killed in a firefight with the British.

Every rebellion needs a martyr, and Qassam proved to be an ideal one for the Arabs. Before his death Qassam wrote a special prayer to God and hid it in his headdress. His funeral became a special exaltation for rebellion against both the British and the Jews. The guerrillas that he inspired were nationalistic idealists reinforced by some common criminals. They wandered from village to village carrying their guns and supplies on mules. Although these bands had no organization or command structure, they nevertheless inspired the Arab population. Qassam is still memorialized today by rockets bearing his name.

Soon the rebels began to attack Jews in the larger urban centers. Life for the Jewish pioneers began to assume a defensive posture against the ever-increasing terror. Bombs were thrown, fields were burnt, telephone cables were cut, electric poles were toppled, bridges were blown up, and roads were blocked. The country was coming to a standstill.

A particular striking episode of the Arab revolt was the massacre at the Edison Theatre in Jerusalem. Three persons were shot dead and two others were hurt by an unknown assassin who shot point blank into a crowd leaving the movie theatre. A warning letter called the murders "a war of extermination against the Jews."

The Arab revolt continued the violence against the Jewish community in Palestine as eighteen people were hurt in a bomb blast on a Haifa train on June 14, 1936.

On Thursday, July 30, 1936, the Peel Commission was announced, with broad powers to restore order to Mandate Palestine. Orders for martial law in Palestine were issued at the same time as the bishop of Jerusalem and the chief rabbi of Agudath Israel, an Orthodox group, both appealed for peace. On November 26, 1936, Chaim Weizman issued his famous quote "that there are 6,000,000 Jews who are condemned to be penned up in places where they cannot live and where they are not wanted."

The Arab Higher Committee established a nationalist government of Palestinian Arabs. The Grand Mufti Husseini decided to firmly back the revolt. In addition to the violence, a general strike was declared. The strike that began in April 1936 lasted six long months. The strike was not uniformly adhered to, as many thought that their jobs would be taken by new Jewish immigrants. As in many Arab events, the strike and the rebellion soon degenerated into internecine Arab fighting. Many took the opportunity to murder members of opposing clans and tribes under the cover of the rebellion and strike. Several Arab leaders were murdered as a result of blood feuds and family violence.

In spite of the internal fighting, the Arab community had made a clear point. It wanted independence both from the British and the Jews. It proved that the Palestinian Arab community could be an important force.

The British put down the rebellion with uncommon ferocity. Airplanes with machine guns attacked the marauding bands and numerous Arab houses were blown up on the pretext that they sheltered snipers. Citrus groves by the hundreds were burnt. Checkpoints sprung up everywhere to guard against guerrilla infiltration. Many Arabs were hanged by the British authorities. Unfortunately the State of Israel learned only too well the lessons that the British had taught them in order to put down rebellions.

By the 1930s, in the second decade of the British Mandate more than 250,000 Jews had settled in Palestine. The Chancellorship of Adolf Hitler and his obsession with the Jews had initially proved to be a great impetus for Jewish settlement and immigration. Now the time for reckoning had come. What would the British do in view of the tide of Jewish immigration and the resultant Arab rebellion?

The Arab rebellion had convinced the British authorities that there was no hope for Arab and Jews to live together in a single community. In the summer of 1936, the Peel Commission was convened. After months of hearings where such notables as Chaim Weizman, David Ben-Gurion, Jabotinsky, Husseini, Winston Churchill, and David Lloyd George all testified, it was clear what the decision would be—partition.

Ben-Gurion stated that the Bible was the Jewish people's "Mandate." The Grand Mufti Husseini, the chief Palestinian leader, clearly enunciated the premise that there was no chance for co-existence between the two peoples.

The Peel Commission's report would divide British Mandate Palestine into Arab and Jewish enclaves with the British holding Jerusalem and a narrow corridor to the sea.

To say that neither side was happy is an understatement. The Arabs in particular were vehemently opposed to a plan recognizing any Jewish rights. The Yishuv's leadership under Ben-Gurion and Weizman were inclined to accept the partition despite strong opposition from both the Jewish left and right.

Eventually new commissions were created and the acrimonious debate continued. Commensurate with the arguments over partition were the incessant Arab terrorism against the Jews and the increasing Jewish immigration from Europe. As war approached, it became apparent to the British that they must stop the influx of Jews.

A final prewar conference was held at St James' Palace in London. The Jews and Arabs would not sit together, and the major Arab clans, the Husseinis and Nashashibis, would not sit with one another.

At the conference, Malcolm McDonald, the British foreign secretary who had previously been a friend to Ben-Gurion, ordered that Jewish immigration be severely curtailed. The limit was to be 75,000 immigrants for the next five years, after which it was to be completely stopped. Neville Chamberlain, the British Prime Minister, said, "If we must offend one side then let us offend the Jews rather than the Arabs."

The lead headline in the *Palestine Post* of November 11, 1938, read, "Nazi hooligans vent wrath on Jews throughout Germany." Most of the front page of the paper dealt with what we now know as Kristallnacht.

In March 1939, when Hitler tore up the Munich agreement and annexed the remainder of Czechoslovakia, Palestine was preoccupied with the final report of the Royal Peel Commission. It was ordained, as predicted, that Arab land sales to Jews as well as Jewish migration to Palestine were to be severely curtailed. The Yishuv correctly predicted that there would be an ongoing political struggle against the British administration.

As the Jewish people gazed into the horrible abyss that was to become World War II and the Holocaust, they must have known that many, too many, of their people would be doomed. The stage was now set for the British blockade of Palestine.

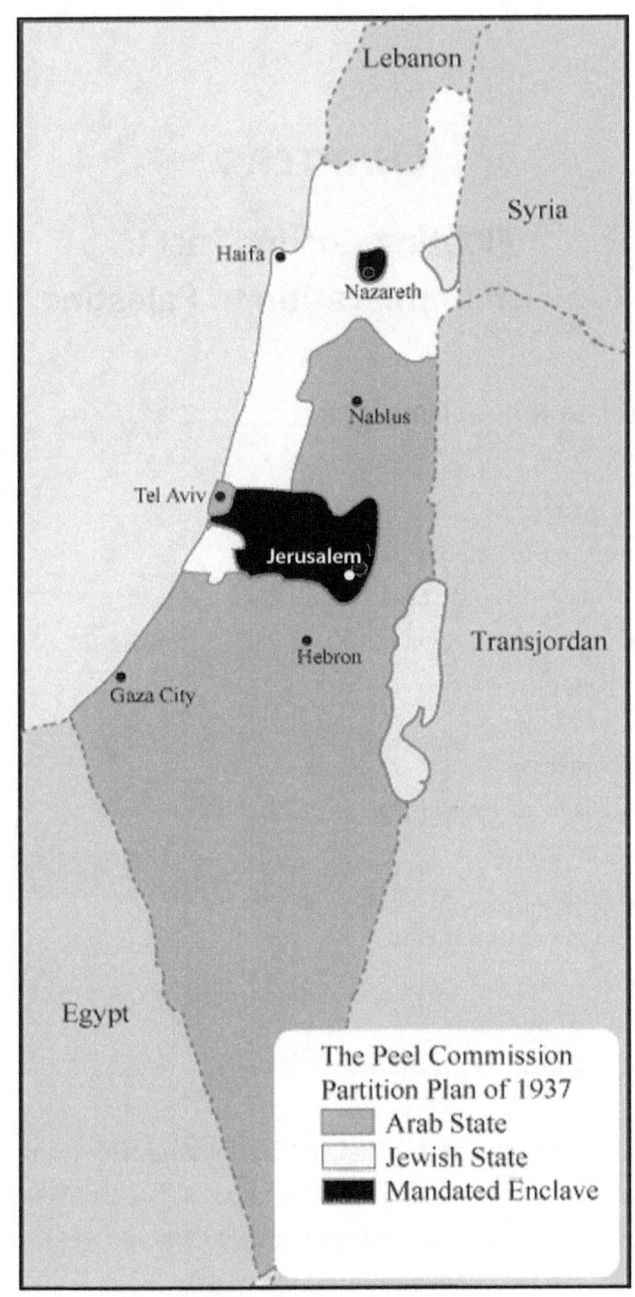

Peel Commission Boundaries

CHAPTER 2

Floating Coffins Part I: Jewish Immigration to Palestine

Song of the Illegal Immigrant

It does not matter
Brother from where you came
Or why to board this moving deck
Crammed from hole to smokestack
It's a battleship this wreck
Though it has no guns
We warriors thereon
Though we have no arms of iron
Yet we have an iron will
Against all odds
To build the future of our land
Win we shall!
Our nation and our land
We shall make them live again.

Jewish immigration to British Mandate Palestine after Hitler came to power in 1933 can be roughly divided into three phases. The first comprised the waves of Jewish immigrants from Germany and then Austria up until 1936.

Austrian Jews began to leave en masse after the Anschluss in March 1938. The Arab revolt started in 1936, and the British began their infamous blockade. The second period was almost entirely illegal and subject to the quotas that the British authorities imposed. This second period lasted through the war years, when few, if any, managed to run the cordon of the British naval blockade. A third phase occurred in the postwar years from 1945 until 1948 and the declaration of independence by Israel. This period was marked by intense activity against the British, motivated by the desire not only to populate Palestine with Jews but also to embarrass the British and eventually force them to leave.

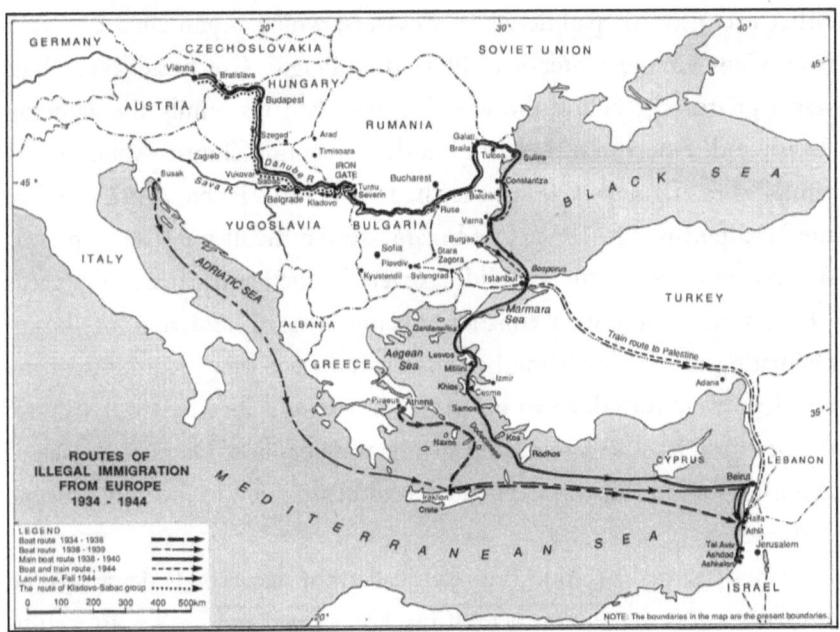

Israeli historical accounts of the fight against the British blockade must be weighted for the biases of the Israeli right, the Revisionists and the Israeli political left. [2] Both sides are quick to claim victories and great accomplishments while denying responsibility for tragic errors.

---

[2]   The Revisionists were a right-wing political party that felt that the future Jewish homeland must encompass all of Palestine.

Any reasonable analysis will show that the majority of ships that ran the blockade before the war were launched and funded by the Revisionists.

The very first account of a ship that came ashore was a Revisionist sailboat, the *Kosta*. It came all the way from Vienna down the Danube and eventually landed sixteen illegal immigrants on Palestinian shores in March 1937. They simply waded ashore with no landing organization in place. As 1937 ran into 1938, the number of passengers increased, as did the size and sophistication of the ships and the landing arrangements.

A favourite route for the illegal ships was down the Danube River from Vienna into the Black Sea and then on to the Mediterranean through the Dardanelles and the Sea of Marmora. Hans Klein was on one of three ships, either excursion or paddle-wheel steamers, which began such a voyage from Vienna in the winter of 1939. Born in Prague, Czechoslovakia, Hans was a pharmacist before the war. He described his family life as being Jewish and respectful of Judaism but definitely not Zionist. Although his family were originally Czechs, they had moved to Vienna, Austria, before the Nazi takeover in 1938. Life became very difficult for Jews in prewar Austria, as visits to official buildings were banned and strict ration cards were issued. People were constantly being arrested, and rumours began circulating about Jews being beaten. Curfews at 8 p.m. became the rule, and Jews were forbidden to go to the movies and theatre. Even visits to the beautiful forests surrounding Vienna were banned. Despite the lack of Zionism, for many it was a time to flee and Palestine was the only possible destination.

Hans boarded a ship in Bratislava called the *Uranus*. He described the embarkation as tremendously exciting. The *Uranus* and its two sister ships preparing to sail down the Danube had been chartered by a Jewish agency simply called the Joint. All they could bring onboard was a knapsack with a few personal possessions. People embraced their close friends and relatives. At the last moment a few panicked and decided not to go. Even those Jews on the ships who did not have a Zionist orientation decided to pursue the only course available to them and take the difficult journey to Palestine.

Klein described the three ships sailing together. The three hundred passengers crowded on one ship slept together on the dining room floor. They always seemed to get enough food, but there were minimal facilities, so the food was heated on the floor of the dining room. The Danube froze over and the three bands of intrepid Jewish refugees were stuck for the rest of the winter in the ice. Nearby Yugoslavian Jews in the tiny port of Tradova came over the ice on skis to aid their co-religionists. There was no water available, so the passengers ventured onto the frozen river and chopped holes into the ice, melted it, and finally had drinking water.

Cleanliness and privacy were almost nonexistent. The chopped ice was also boiled to provide some water for washing, but there were no showers. Somehow the captain's cabin was warm, although the rest of the passengers were described as being blue with the cold. The captain took a fancy to one attractive girl, and she made it into the warm cabin. Whatever cabins were available were usually jammed with people. A few lucky ones had beds, but most passengers slept on floors, shivering. Basic amenities could be acquired in exchange for services. A so-called stewardess on the ship went to the nearby town and acquired some material for a dress. Alise Hans, an excellent dressmaker, sewed her, as she described it, a fine dress. Suddenly warm water appeared in payment for the dress.

Almost everyone remembered their embarkation on these and other ships. For many it was the first time they saw their transportation in broad daylight. Leaky, creaky old ships, some of them converted excursion boats or ferries, were going to be their salvation. Overcrowded, dank, rotting, and filled with vermin, these were the lifeboats for the Jews of Europe.

The embarkations were always filled with surprises. Sam Shene described his and his two older sisters' embarkation just after the war ended. As they waited in a very long line they were approached by a hysterical Hassidic man. He tapped the older sister on the back and asked her to take his suitcase onboard. The three children had the precious immigration certificates. They were legal. The Hassidic man, who was trembling and near hysteria, had no certificate. He handed them the heavy suitcase.

The remnants of the Shene family made their way up the gangplank dragging the heavy suitcase. Their parents were dead and the three orphans looked forward to a new life in Palestine. Finally they got on board with their meagre possessions. The three teenagers were anxious, wondering what they had brought onboard. Was it a Torah, gold, money, a religious artefact? They opened the suitcase and noticed the air holes. The suitcase contained a little boy struggling to get out. He was a typical Hassidic child with earlocks and *tzitis* (prayer shawl fringes). The three children sat down and cried. They had saved a little boy. He was going to Palestine with them.

Almost all refugee immigrants described their embarkation as chaotic. The Jewish agencies and Zionist groups tried their best under extreme circumstances, but the pressure and desperation of those that were fleeing many times overcame even the best organization. One can only picture crowds of frantic people, sometimes in fear of British authorities, other times fleeing the Nazis and still other times being victimized by gangsters preying on them, pushing and shoving their way onto the congested gangplank.

Sometimes men disguised themselves as pregnant women or used baby carriages as a subterfuge. Many times illegal immigrants were able to board with the legal ones due to the tumult. One Jewish man impersonated a priest and was virtually beaten to death by the port authorities. Another had no shoes and still another, a girl, smuggled small gold jewellery in the hem of her dress. Besides the fear many were filled with remorse because of lost relatives or loved ones.

Luggage was an enormous problem with so many people jammed into spaces meant for so few. Most situations found the passengers only able to take what they could carry in knapsacks or rucksacks. Many times they were allowed luggage only to have it jettisoned into the water. Numerous other times the luggage that was supposed to arrive never did. These precious pieces of luggage were the last possessions of refugees fleeing the Nazis or Holocaust survivors trying to restart their lives.

A Holocaust survivor named Laslo Leung described his embarkation on an illegal immigration transport ship named the *Hagannah* in 1946. Three thousand people gathered in a secret location to depart. Most of these Jewish refugees and survivors were young Romanians and Hungarians desperate to flee Europe. Laslo's knapsack contained all his worldly possessions: two pairs of socks, two sets of underwear, and a worn pair of shoes. His most precious possession was a $20 US bill that he kept clutched to him. His cousin had given him the precious bill to enable him to restart his life in Jewish Palestine.

The *Hagannah* was so decrepit that the pier was higher than the ship, forcing the passengers to make their way down to the ship on a rickety ladder. Laslo confronted bunks similar to those in Auschwitz. The ship was so crowded that many had to sleep on the deck. When they ran out of gasoline they cut up the bunks and fed the wood to the boiler. It was July 1946, and the weather was indescribably hot. Those sleeping in the lower depths of the ship were constantly thirsty and many collapsed from heat exhaustion. Nevertheless the people were mostly happy. They talked of their new lives, a possible new country. They talked, they slept, and they ate, but they did not know what to expect. In contrast to other ships, there was no singing or dancing and no flags, but they had a purpose.

Another prospective Palestinian immigrant named Alexander Eisen boarded an illegal ship in Sète, France, near Marseille in April 1946. His first sense of the ship as he struggled up the gangplank was the smell. The ship also contained the Auschwitz-like bunks. Alexander had been the last one up the gangplank, but besides the smell he immediately felt the adrenaline. This was a ship filled with Zionist songs and *hora* dancing. The flag that was designed by David Wolfson at the first Zionist Congress in 1897, the future Israeli flag, was everywhere. The blue Star of David on a white background with the two blue horizontal stripes became a powerful symbol for these tortured people, survivors of the Holocaust and refugees from the vast prison camp that had been Nazi occupied Europe. As Alexander described it, the passengers sang, danced, studied, and played chess. But above all they celebrated their passage to their new home and country.

Another Holocaust survivor, Jacob Steindler, who had belonged to the left-wing Zionist party Hashomer Hatzair, described being packed like sardines into a tiny fishing boat for his journey in 1946. Steindler, a Hungarian Jew, had always aspired to go to Israel. He had been inspired by Hannah Senesch and other Zionists who had parachuted into Hungary and Yugoslavia. While the captain of the fishing boat was from the Haganah organization, the rest of the crew were not Jewish. The engine of the small vessel broke down and the crew ran away with their money and supplies. The desperate group spent three weeks adrift on the Mediterranean before they were apprehended by a British coastal patrol boat and towed to Cyprus, where they were incarcerated for the rest of 1946.

Jacob Goldstein was born in Lodz, Poland, to a traditional Jewish family. His grandfather, a quasi-architect, was intensely Zionistic. In 1940, Jacob found himself imprisoned in the Lodz ghetto but managed to survive to be deported to Auschwitz in 1944 with members of his family. He was separated from his family after being examined by the infamous Dr. Mengele. Jacob survived the inspection only by claiming to be much older than he was. After ten days in Auschwitz, Jacob was sent on a death march. He related how many brave people stood and threw bread at the struggling marchers.

Jacob was liberated by American troops some two kilometres from the Russian zone. As he was starving, he ate horsemeat and drank liquor from an abandoned German vehicle. The American soldiers showered Jacob with chocolate bars and cigarettes. Goldstein remembered the soldiers literally emptying their pockets to give him everything they could. He described himself as gaunt and emaciated, with his clothes in tatters.

Jacob then found his way to the Russian zone so that he could return home. The Russian soldiers embraced him and told him, "Tovarich (comrade), take whatever you want, loot the German village." Goldstein met Russian soldiers from Mongolia who he felt were very primitive. The Mongolians seemed to delight in stealing watches, and most of them sported four or five on each arm. Feeling cold, Jacob started a fire with a nearby crate, not knowing that it was filled with thousands of Deutsch marks. He only found the charred remains later.

Goldstein then found himself in Stettlin on the Baltic and rode the roof of a train to get back to his family home in Lodz. After finding no one alive, he threaded his way through absolute chaos to try and get to Prague. Along the way he was arrested and spent several days in Katowice, Poland.

Jacob learned of the Bricha (the flight of European Jewry) and made his way to an assembly point at a Catholic convent in Pilsen. All his worldly possessions were in a rucksack and a blanket and he had no identification papers. Finally, after a torturous journey through Landsbergh, Bavaria he ended up in a UNRRA camp.* From there Jacob continued his journey and found himself in Grifenberg, Bavaria, which was a Hascharah kibbutz.³ He was brought together with 150-160 Jewish boys and girls who all had a transformative moment as they met soldiers from the Jewish Brigade. The Star of David shoulder patches mesmerised the teenagers, and they all openly wept. Goldstein stayed in Grifenberg until 1946.

The Jewish Agency organized 150 trucks to transport the teenagers from Grifenberg to Marseille. The Bricha set up cultural activities, which included teaching them Hebrew. The youngsters had a literal Tower of Babel as they spoke to each other in Yiddish, Polish, German, Russian, and the newly taught Hebrew. They all spent four to five months in Marseille as the Bricha prepared an illegal immigrant ship. It was clear it would be illegal, as none of them had the precious immigration certificates. It was also clear that the French authorities knew exactly what was happening and were perfectly willing to defy the British authorities.

Still another Holocaust survivor, Louis Stulowicz, told his story of leaving Marseille, France, in late 1947 and trying to arrive in Israel and aid in the 1948 War of Independence. Fourteen hundred people together with numerous arms and ammunitions, even tanks, were jammed on a ship meant for a maximum of seven hundred people. His passage involved many problems with people's behaviour as the passengers fought amongst themselves. Food and drinking water were too scarce and the lack of washing facilities made everyone very irritable. There are many stories of the embarkations and attempted passages to Palestine, but common threads run through them all. Almost all the ships were unseaworthy. They were old vessels with engines that frequently broke down and sometimes couldn't be repaired. There was never enough food or water, and washing

---

³   Hascharah were collective places which prepared people for life in Palestine.
*   Unrra United Nations relief organization.

facilities were nonexistent. They had to attempt hazardous voyages across hostile waters. Not only did they have to avoid the Nazis and their allies the Romanians and the Italians, but they also had to break the British blockade and keep these heroic people moving forward.

Another memory that lives on besides the embarkations was the train travel to get to the embarkation ports. Automobile travel for the Jews in Nazi-occupied Europe was nonexistent and impossible. After the war Jewish agencies, Zionist groups and the Joint cooperated in transporting the Holocaust survivors en masse in truck convoys to the embarkation ports. Clearly this was not possible until the Nazis were defeated. The memory of some Jews impersonating Gentiles and using fake papers during the war was indelibly stamped on all their consciousness.

The images of the Gestapo and SS sauntering through the train checking papers are etched into our memories from the many movies of the period. One such account in an archival memoir told of a Hungarian Jewish family, the Mayers, consisting of two parents and a three-year-old girl travelling on a train from Hungary through Romania in an effort to get to the Black Sea port of Constanza. From there they hoped to get onboard an illegal immigrant ship, run the British blockade, and start a new life for themselves and their young daughter. They carried carefully doctored false passports, as well as exit visas to Bolivia.

Everyone exiting Romania needed an exit visa. Fraudulent exit visas were easy to obtain for most South American countries, like Bolivia. Only the most incompetent and idiotic Romanian immigration officials would not realize the deception. Who could go to Bolivia though the Black Sea? But the Mayer family were well prepared; they had American currency and gold jewellery to grease the palms of the hapless officials. The Mayers were prepared for all eventualities except language. Being Hungarian, they spoke only a few words of Romanian. They sat terrified and praying that their limited vocabulary would suffice for the passport check. Their three-year-old daughter, Astrid, sat between them transfixed by the train and the moving scenery.

Soon the doors to their compartment burst open. A tall SS officer in a grey uniform with the usual SS embellishments looked in at the terrified and quiet threesome. He approached their daughter and said in German, "*Vos es dar noome ma sheina kitn?*" What is your name my little darling child?

"*Ich bin Madeline*," the precocious little child said. I am Madeline.

The SS officer pinched the little girl's cheek and moved on to the next compartment. The three-year-old child's endless rehearsals of the few words of German had paid off; they were saved.

Amri Sussman described his journey by train in 1944. A traditional Jew who belonged to Mizrachi, the religious Zionist organization, Amri made his way from Czechoslovakia to Budapest, Hungary. Many Hungarian Jews were conscripted into labour battalions to aid the army. They were sent to the Eastern front to fight against the Russians amidst appalling conditions. Few Jews survived the cold, deprivations, and harsh treatment of the Eastern front. Luckily Amri, using false papers and a faked baptismal certificate, was able to avoid conscription.

Amri was able to connect with Rezo Kastner and get on the Kastner transport.[4] They were some 1300 people on the train. German officials had been bribed and the train, filled with desperate people, was destined eventually for Switzerland. The railroad lines were constantly bombed by Allied planes. To add to the chaos, some of the passengers were from Poland. They became absolutely hysterical with the thoughts that the train was going to Auschwitz. Paranoia enveloped the train's passengers as to which direction it was going. The Red Cross approached the train at a stop and the entire train was disinfected. Eventually a few hundred passengers made it to Switzerland. Others were interned at Bergen-Belsen but kept in separate quarters from the main camp.

Sussman arrived in Switzerland after a torturous and convoluted journey. They were sequestered as illegal refugee immigrants and spent six months there. The Red Cross provided a little assistance, but the British would not issue the Palestine immigration certificates. There was much talk that they would be deported either to Mauritius or Madagascar.

---

[4]   The Kastner Transport was a train that transported more than 1,300 Jews from Hungary to safety after bribing German officers in June 1944.

Apparently, only the very rich or very Zionist got the immigration certificates. Finally the British authorities provided the necessary papers.

Somehow the Kastner train passengers acquired some money, which they needed to bribe German officers. The war was winding down, and German officials were only too happy to take money and possibly ingratiate themselves to the survivors and other officials. The Kastner train, lubricated by bribery, made its way from Montreaux, Switzerland, to Tarrento in northern Italy. Here the astonished Jewish refugees met soldiers from the Jewish Brigade. By spreading around the names of his family, Sussman was able to find his brother, wife, and younger sister. Eventually Amri found a ship to board and after a somewhat chaotic embarkation departed for Haifa.

Another Zionist youth group member, Eri Neuman, described a "Beta" (an illegal) train from Vienna, Austria, to Zagreb, Yugoslavia, in March 1938. The train was jammed with Jews attempting at any cost to flee Vienna after the Nazi takeover. Neuman's fondest memory was the entire Zagreb Jewish community turning out to greet the train at its stop. The scene at the train stop was a momentous event in Neuman's life. The train was surrounded by rings of armed Yugoslavian soldiers. Nevertheless the entire Zagreb Jewish community came to shout, "Shalom!" Meat, cheese, wine, salami, and even sardines were pushed through the armed guards to the grateful passengers. People were crying, praying, and blessing all at the same time. The crowd pushed through little pieces of paper with prayers as well as good wishes. The authorities stopped similar demonstrations at Belgrade. When the train reached prewar Greece, the authorities hustled the train through at high speed.

Some of the train passengers were Zionists, while others were Orthodox Jews simply fleeing the Nazis. Neuman described the train as being very politically divided, with constant squabbles between the Bundists (socialists), Zionists, and Orthodox all carving out their territories. Eventually Neuman made his way to prewar Palestine, running the British blockade.

The train journeys and the embarkations were only a prelude to the sea voyages. Once onboard the passengers faced an uncertain fate. Depending on the timing, they faced either the Nazis or the British, who anxious to stop them at all costs. Many faced both.

CHAPTER 3

The Floating Coffins Part II:
The Voyages at Sea

Those immigrants who departed in the months and few years before the Second World War and those who attempted to come after or during the war experienced some similarities and many differences in their immigration experiences. In both cases, and through perhaps the entire period from 1936 to 1948, the British attempts to stop Jewish immigration were a major factor. Those who came in the prewar years embarked from Black Sea ports, like Constanza and Tulcea in Romania, and came from places like Vienna to sail down the Danube. In the postwar period the ports of Marseille and Sète in France, as well as ports like Bari in Italy, were the prime embarkation points.

When the Jewish immigrants reached the sea, whether it was the Mediterranean or the Black Sea, regardless of the timing, they all commented on their end goal of coming to the sea. They breathed the salty air and saw the seagulls and waves crashing ashore. Salvation and immigration to the Promised Land were at hand. Not a few waded into the water and splashed around, hoping that their long journeys were coming to an end. A few days at sea and they would be in Palestine.

One of the most interesting aspects of the blockade is the naming of the many ships. In many ways they signify the vast ideological spectrum that existed within the Zionist movement. Some ships were named after Israeli Labour leaders like the *Chaim Alorosoloff*, another after a British labour leader sympathetic to the Jews, the *Josiah Wedgewood*. Another was named after Henrietta Szold, founder of the Hadassah movement. Theodore Herzl, the founder of modern Zionism, inspired a ship name.

Hannah Snesch had a ship in her name as well. And so it went until the memorable *Exodus 1947*, a ship name that seemed to inspire the world about the Israeli cause in 1947.

Despite the many difficulties, the illegal immigrants pressed on. Obstacles like the British blockade and the Nazi threat were swept aside by the desire to get to Palestine. Many improvisations and daring deeds marked the passage to Palestine. One illegal ship, the *Parita,* left from Danzig, Poland, just before the war broke out on September 1, 1939, carrying a cargo of Polish Jewish refugees. The brave passengers led by Revisionist Zionists broke through the British blockade and ran the ship ashore on the beach at Tel Aviv on August 23, 1939. The populace of Tel Aviv were prepared, and thousands streamed onto the beach as the approximately seven hundred passengers quickly scrambled ashore. The crowds mingled with the fleeing refugees and quickly exchanged clothing, beach towels, and other items. Soon the illegal immigrants were safe from the hapless British authorities and their quotas.

The *Parita* was only one of several ships that simply beached themselves on the shores of Palestine. Two illegal ships, the *Gepo II* and the *Katina*, left Vienna, Austria, in the winter of 1939. Each of the ships carried more than seven hundred Jewish refugees and both made their way down the Danube to exit into the Black Sea at the Romanian port of Tulcea. From there the fleeing refugees made their way through the Dardanelles and on into the Mediterranean. The *Gepo II* sank in the Mediterranean, while the *Katina* was lucky enough to be nearby and save the passengers. All fifteen hundred passengers were deposited on the beaches of Netanya and somehow avoided the British authorities.

By this time the desire to escape Nazi-controlled Austria was strong amongst the Jewish population. Soon after the Nazi annexation of Austria in 1938, Adolf Eichmann, who had been responsible for organizing the mass deportations of the Jews in Eastern Europe, arrived in Vienna. Eichmann had been to Palestine twice to study the Jews in, as he put it, "their native habitat," gaining a basic understanding of Jewish customs and religious practices. He soon put this knowledge to good use in Vienna, as he established a processing centre for Jews. It was almost an assembly line procedure, as wealthy Austrian Jews entered one door of the forbidding SS headquarters and emerged penniless at the exit door. They were stripped of their wealth in exchange for precious exit visas and the ability to flee their homeland. The only possible destination for these Jews was Palestine, and they still did not have their immigration certificates. The British authorities, despite the Nazi plans, rigidly enforced their quotas. The distraught Jews resorted to any means necessary to escape and run the British blockade, which seemed to them like a minor obstacle.

Countless other ships and boats in this period attempted to break the British cordon around Palestine. While some were private, as mentioned, most in the prewar period were sent by the right-wing Revisionists. Some were captured by the British and sent back to their embarkation points like Constanza, Romania. Other ships, like the *Assimi*, which left Constanza in March 1939, were captured by the British, turned back to Palestine, and finally managed to land in June 1939.

Countless and varied stories have emerged from this epic tale of determination. One ship carrying more than 600 people left Marseille, France, in March 1939 had more than 400 people evade British arrest while 173 were arrested. Of the 173 arrested passengers, 44 managed to flee custody.

Some of the crews and in particular the commanding officers and captains were imprisoned by the British for lengthy periods. In other cases, some passengers were released after short imprisonments. One ship, the *Rim*, which left Romania near the end of June 1939, caught fire off the island of Rhodes. Fortunately another Greek-based illegal ship rescued the passengers and landed both complements of passengers near Netanya two months later, near the end of August 1939.

A very large ship, the *Tiger Hill*, left Romania on the eve of war in mid-August 1939. It carried fourteen hundred passengers, an assortment of Jewish refugees from Poland, Bulgaria, and Czechoslovakia. As the ship reached the Palestinian shore on September 1, 1939, a British patrol ship fired on the *Tiger Hill*. The two Jewish refugees who were shot during the incident were probably the first persons killed by British forces during the war, which had only begun that day with the British declaration of war on Germany after the invasion of Poland. On September 3, 1939, only two days after the onset of the war, the *Tiger Hill* managed to beach itself on the Tel Aviv shore and most of the fourteen hundred passengers were able to scramble ashore and mingle with crowds of rescuers and onlookers. Three of the refugees were killed on the beach as the British Marine Patrol fired on the migrants.

On September 19, 1939, a ship called the *Noemi Julia* sailed directly into Haifa harbour and demanded admission to Palestine for those on board. Following the British public relations debacle of the *Tiger Hill* shootings just weeks before, British authorities relented and all the illegal immigrants were allowed ashore.

Only a few of the so-called floating coffins attempted the run against the British blockade for the balance of the fall of 1939. In early 1940, a major endeavour was mounted by the right-wing Revisionists. A very large and fast ship, the *Sakarya*, carrying more than 2000 illegal immigrants, attempted to cross the blockade. The ship was commanded by Eri Jabotinsky, son of Vladamir Zeev Jabotinsky, the legendary head of the right-wing Revisionist Zionist movement. The *Sakarya* flew the neutral Turkish flag and was soon sighted near the Palestinian coast. British patrol ships intercepted the *Sakarya* and escorted it into Haifa harbour. Of the 2,176 refugees aboard, more than eight hundred were women and children. Some fourteen hundred of the passengers held German passports or other travel documents. Several hundred immigrants held Hungarian passports, while many held visas for unlikely destinations like Bolivia, Liberia, and China. More than one thousand passengers had travel documents with no visas at all. None of the passengers had British immigration certificates for Palestine. During this period, anyone travelling in Europe needed a passport and an exit visa to a destination country. All of the passengers were taken ashore and immediately interned in the British concentration camp Atlit. Eri Jabotinsky was put in jail at Akko, another British camp, and kept there for over six months, until his father, Zeev Jabotinsky, died in August 1940.

The British reacted strongly to what they saw as yet another Zionist provocation. They seemed to forget that these were Jews fleeing what was to become the Nazi killing machine. The British decided on an all-out war against illegal Jewish immigration. A Contraband Control Service was established to control and intercept ships carrying illegal immigrants to

Palestine. Despite the contravention of maritime rights, the British pressed ahead. The excuse was used that there might be enemy agents secreted amongst the many women and children. Another reason for barring the Jewish immigrants from landing was the possibility that these terrified refugees were carrying illicit cargo for German agents.

The British tried every diplomatic and coercive means to harass and stop the flow of Jews to Palestine. Ships marooned on the frozen Danube, filled with starving and diseased Jewish men, women, and children, were denied aid. More than a thousand Jewish refugees blocked by the thick ice on the Danube were stuck at the river port of Kladovo, Yugoslavia, in 1940. These people were starving and disease ridden. Appeals were made to the American Jewish Joint Distribution Committee for food and other aid. Yet the British Colonial Office applied pressure to prevent aid from reaching the despairing refugees. Finally the British Foreign Office decided that this tactic would not help American public opinion towards Britain during its time of need in the war. Nevertheless no aid ever reached the Kladovo group. They were marooned in the ice and eventually imprisoned by the Yugoslavians. When the Germans invaded Yugoslavia in April 1941, the one thousand Jewish refugees of Kladovo were all murdered by the Nazis.

The British used every possible diplomatic measure to pressure countries against aiding Jewish illegal immigration to Palestine. In February 1940, the Yugoslavian government, which had not yet been attacked by the Germans and was still neutral, was persuaded to ensure that all passports of Jews embarking on Yugoslavian vessels had a large red "J" stamped on them. One can only imagine how Jews sailing on Yugoslavian ships felt. The British Ambassador in Belgrade sent a note of thanks to the Yugoslavian government for implementing this odious policy.

The Panamanian government was required to cancel the Panamanian registration of ships that were used for illegal immigration. The Liberian government was asked by the British government to stop fraudulent visas being issued. The Paraguayan authorities were asked if the exit visas issued in Prague were valid. Pressure was even placed on Jewish relief organizations in Britain and America to stop all aid to Jews seeking to enter Palestine.

In the midst of all this coercive pressure on far-flung places, Britain was fighting a war against the fearsome Nazi war machine. After the fall of France, in May 1940, Britain was alone and isolated for almost a year. Yet this same Britain fighting for its very life had time to worry about deporting a few Hungarian Jews who had stayed illegally for too long in British Mandate Palestine. Fines and other strictures were imposed, and diplomatic and political pressure continued. Yet the desperation of those Jews who had even a slim chance to flee aroused little British sympathy.

One anti-immigrant operation involved a small ship that was stopped by a British patrol boat just off the Palestinian shore. Just as the British naval vessel approached, a twelve-year-old shinnied up the main mast and fastened the blue and white Star of David flag to the rigging. As the British naval vessel drew alongside, some twenty Jewish youths jumped off the side of the schooner and attempted to swim to shore to nearby Haifa. Undeterred, the British retrieved the swimmers and forced them on board. Eventually they were taken to Cyprus.

The distraught Jews of Europe tried every possible means of escape, even in their floating coffins. However, pursued by the Nazis and blockaded by the British, most Jews of Europe were doomed. Frida Weller described her journey from Sweden in the winter of 1946 as going from hardship to hardship. The ship was barely adequate, clearly unsafe, and not fit for human beings. Frida surmised that it had been a transport ship of some sort, probably meant for carrying animals, not people. The conditions aboard were terrible, and to compound the difficulties the ocean was very rough. As a result, for almost the entire voyage everyone was constantly seasick.

After six long weeks they arrived in Palestine only to be confronted by the British Navy. By this point the engine had failed, and in order to cope, passengers threw everything overboard. Frida cried as she described the loss of even her precious family pictures. Everyone on the ship kept only what they had on their bodies. The British confrontation produced a large fight, an armed struggle, as Frida described it. Eventually the British prevailed, and the decrepit vessel was towed to Cyprus. Zipora Muller related her 1946 journey, which started in Yugoslavia. Zipora was a Hungarian Jew who belonged to Hashomer Hatzair, a left-wing Zionist group. In order to prepare for Palestine, she went into Hachshara, a preparatory type of kibbutz in Europe. She learned some Hebrew, sang some songs, and danced some *horas*.

The illegal refugees then spent their last moments in a forest avoiding British surveillance. Finally they boarded their ship of salvation, which Zipora described as a large fishing boat. Two thousand people were packed in like herrings. Like so many other illegal transports to the Mandate, the ship developed difficulties as it reached the Palestinian coast. In this case it simply sprang a leak. Again all the passengers' belongings were thrown overboard. Then the British naval commandos boarded the vessel, which was barely afloat. The immigrants were completely surrounded and resistance was futile against the heavily armed British. The two thousand illegal immigrants were towed to the Mandate coast. As the British refused to allow them to disembark, all the passengers went on a hunger strike. Finally, after two difficult weeks, the British command relented and the entire group disembarked onto a convoy of trucks and were taken to a British concentration camp in Palestine, presumably Atlit. After three months of imprisonment they were finally allowed into British Mandate Palestine.

In August 1946, several illegal immigrant ships arrived in Palestine. Amongst them were the *Yagur* and the *Henrietta Szold*. In preparation to deport the refugees, the British cleared the cargo jetties and piers and set up wire cages to hold detained immigrants. Two ships were readied for the trip to Cyprus, the *Empire Rival* and the *Wedgewood*. The authorities had concluded that the blockade would continue and that Jewish refugees attempting entry into Palestine would be detained and deported. Some of these ships arrived without drinking water, and some desperate passengers drank water from the sea. Subsequently they became mad with dehydration and had to be restrained.

One ship, the *Four Freedoms*, packed with more than one thousand illegal immigrants, was intercepted by the British patrol vessels in September 3, 1946. As was typical, the ship was rammed by two British destroyers and extensive damage was caused to its superstructure. The *Four Freedoms* was flying the Zionist flag, and the British ordered that the flag be lowered immediately. The passengers and crew refused, and journalists nearby saw that the ship was then sprayed with machine-gun fire. The migrants responded by standing on the deck and singing "Hatikvah," which would become the Israeli national anthem in 1948. When the British Marines attempted to board the *Four Freedoms* they were initially repulsed with water hoses and numerous projectiles thrown at them. Guns were never used by the deportees. The entire group of more than one thousand passengers were then transferred to the *Empire Heywood* and sent to Cyprus.

In 1946, the six-hundred-ton *Josiah Wedgewood* arrived in Haifa. It carried thirteen hundred refugees from Greece, Yugoslavia, Czechoslovakia, and Poland. It also carried a large banner which read, "We survived Hitler. Death is no stranger. Nothing can keep us from out Jewish homeland."

Martin Branak left northern Italy after the end of the war. He found himself on yet another illegal ship. As usual the engine burnt out in the middle of the Mediterranean. The ship drifted under the hot summer sun until the British found them and towed them to Cyprus. There they languished in a series of camps until they were finally allowed to go in to British Mandate Palestine.

Laslo Leung told the story of his voyage on a ship aptly named the *Haganah*. The crew members were part of an elite group named the Palmach who were essential to the continuing efforts to break the British blockade. For this reason, the Palestinian Jewish crew did not want to be captured by the British if boarded and freely mingled with the passengers, carrying no identifying insignia or badges. About 100 kilometres from Haifa they were rammed by British war ships. Cables were attached to the refugee boat and the British began the towing operation. In a frenzy, the distraught passengers bombarded the British with all manner of food, including tinned goods.

The decrepit ship and distraught passengers spent seven very long days moored in the Haifa harbour. The captain and crew disguised themselves as refugees. Others amongst these key Palmach operatives hid in secret prepared receptacles on the ship. When Jewish work crews came aboard to clean and maintain the ship, these operatives mingled with the crews and simply walked off the ship at the end of the work day. Despite stringent British security, no one ever bothered to count the crews. The fact that more workers left the ship than came on was lost on the British command. Every effort was made to save these important personnel and preserve them for future operations.

There were also many pregnant women aboard Leung's ship, as well as a number of Haganah who were men disguised as pregnant women. These also were taken ashore and soon rejoined the illegal immigration effort.

Laslo also commented that after the initial fighting during the boarding, the British were basically non-violent. Indeed, not a few soldiers seemed to be very sympathetic to the Holocaust survivors. In the end those who were not smuggled ashore were taken to Atlit in a convoy of trucks, where they languished for many months in what Laslo described as a British concentration camp. But in Atlit they were still able to dance, sing, and, most importantly, eat.

Alexander Eisen found himself in Sète near Marseille, France, in 1946 awaiting illegal immigration. His eight or nine months in Displaced Persons camps had changed his character, causing him to become very Zionistic. He clearly remembered the cries of the birds and the fish jumping in and out of the water. The salty air of the Mediterranean was like a tonic to him. The bunks on the ship reminded him of Auschwitz, but he conceded the ship and all the procedures were very organized. His journey took two weeks, but because of the horrendous conditions on the ship, this felt more like two years. In fact, all the immigrants interviewed for this book felt that the length of time spent on board these decrepit ships was far greater than it actually was. Extreme hardship always seems to make time pass slower.

In the immediate postwar years, British airplanes were constantly patrolling the Mediterranean scouring it for illegal immigrant ships. Every time an airplane was heard the immigrants would scramble below decks to avoid being seen. Symbols such as Star of David flags and banners had to be quickly hidden, and all signs that the ship was an illegal Jewish immigrant ship were covered. Alex Eisen remembered several times that British patrolling aircraft came over their ship and that the passengers reacted with panic.

Alex Eisen loved electronics, and his most precious possessions were his textbooks about the subject. He spent his time tinkering and trying to build radios. Chess playing became an important hobby for many. Others spent their time studying for future vocations or just reading. As one can imagine, political discussions dominated conversation. Would there be a Jewish state? What form would it take? What was the postwar world going to be like? As usual, heated arguments broke out about politics between the various Zionist factions, the religious and the non-Zionistic socialists.

Jacob Goldstein, the young Holocaust survivor from Auschwitz, embarked on his journey to Palestine in the late summer of 1946 from a beach near a small fishing village adjacent to Marseille. Each youngster had a package consisting of bread and chocolate. The Jewish authorities wanted to pack as many people as possible onto the ship, the *Latrun*, so all the ballast was taken out to enable them to fill the ship with as many of the young Zionists as possible. The gangplank was well organized, and each of the pioneers carried only a rucksack with a few personal possessions.

As the ship began to sail a serious list developed, causing the ship to lean dangerously to one side. Many thought the ship was going to capsize, so everyone began to scream, "*Yemina*!" To the left! So everyone ran to the left. Then everything shifted, and the ship began to lean to the right. "*Smoleh*!" To the right! They shifted again, and so it went until the ship was stabilized.

Jacob Goldstein was given the job of handing out food. He was definitely a take-charge person. As the ship sailed, many former partisans in the hold bean to sing patriotic Hebrew songs. Everyone was plagued with lice, and there was an awful fear of typhoid, so everyone was sprayed with delousing powder. Goldstein reflected that it was ironic that the ship was named after a British prison camp in Palestine.[5] Nevertheless the mood of the people was very elevated as they sensed the end of their long journeys.

---

[5] Latrun is now an Israeli military museum near Jerusalem and was the site of a famous battle in 1948.

As the *Latrun* approached Crete they saw many British warships. Soon they were asked for identification. They immediately raised the Panamanian flag. As soon as they entered the territorial waters of British Mandate Palestine, two British warships rammed the ship and it came to a dead halt. Soon British marines jumped on board and the usual fight ensued. Several British soldiers were thrown overboard, but the British soon seized control of the *Latrun*. Jacob commented that the British soldiers did not seem very happy in their tasks, but like most soldiers they were simply following orders.

The *Latrun* was taken to Haifa harbour where the irate passengers were transferred to the *Ocean Vigour* and then sent to Cyprus. Soon the Zionist youth found themselves in a summer camp on Cyprus. Jacob Goldstein spent seven long months in a Cyprus detention camp. He commented that the British soldiers guarding them were very circumspect and would not react to insults and taunts. While they were on Cyprus the Haganah blew a hole in the *Ocean Vigour*. Subsequently the waters surrounding Cyprus were extensively patrolled by British motorboats to prevent any escape.

Jacob was nineteen years old by now and was very upset with the poor diet. Although not starving, he and the other youths were always hungry. Sympathetic Turks and Cypriots threw oranges over the barbed wire to the imprisoned youth.

In September 1947 Goldstein left Cyprus and was sent to Atlit for a month. From there he made his way to Ashdot and a nearby kibbutz. At the kibbutz he learned Hebrew and began to train for Israel's fight for independence in 1948. The initial training took place with sticks before guns were eventually acquired.

Jacob remembers a battle in 1948 when he threw a Molotov cocktail at a Syrian tank. He also remembers Kol Israel, the voice of Israel, continuously broadcasting the names of those missing from the Holocaust and World War II. The many and varied voyages of the floating coffins exemplify the courage and devotion of tens of thousands of illegal immigrants that tried to break the British blockade.

The refugees on crowded ships remembered the Auschwitz conditions.

Remembering the horrors of train deportations.

PARITA delivered her human cargo by running up on the beach at Tel Aviv during the early hours of August 23, 1939.

The Parita on the beach in Tel-Aviv

Disembarking passengers on the Tel-Aviv beach.

Chapter 4

The *Patria*

One of the most horrendous events to strike the Jewish people and the Zionist movement in the Yishuv was the *Patria* disaster. In September 1940 the British were aware that thousands of Jewish refugees were gathering in the south-eastern parts of Europe. While the mass killings had not yet begun the Jews of Europe were terrified; they had to escape before it was too late.

In addition to some of those who had been marooned on the ice-bound Danube in the winter of 1940, thousands of others made their way south along the broad river. Soon they all assembled at the Romanian port of Tulcea on the Black Sea. The several thousand migrants boarded three Greek cargo ships, which were soon renamed the *Atlantic*, *Pacific*, and *Milos*. These three decrepit vessels ventured out into the Black Sea under Panamanian flag and registry to proceed on their dangerous journey to Palestine. The *Milos* was carrying more than seven hundred passengers, while the *Pacific* carried more than one thousand and the *Atlantic* close to two thousand.

Conditions on the three ships were poor, with one British officer describing them as appalling. The ships were all overcrowded and filthy. The toilet facilities were completely inadequate, forcing people to stand in line for hours. The food provisions were poor, and much of the food was spoiled. The water was almost undrinkable. As a result most of the passengers became sick with diarrhoea and other illnesses. Whenever there was turbulence almost everyone became seasick. To add to these poor conditions there was almost no room to stand. The sick passengers were pressed together like cattle waiting for slaughter.

As the Atlantic passed Istanbul on the way to the Mediterranean the local Jewish community managed to smuggle some food aboard. When the ship reached Crete in October it had no food, fuel, or water left. Subsequently typhoid broke out amongst the crowded passengers. In addition, the Greek captain and crew of the *Atlantic*, frightened by the progress of the war, tried to escape in the only lifeboat available. Luckily the harbour police detained the fleeing crew and ordered them back to their ship. Some coal was supplied and the *Atlantic* moved on.

The desperate passengers broke up wooden parts of the boat and fed them to the boilers to continue their journey. As their odyssey continued, some of the passengers sighted land. They had reached Cyprus. Soon a British launch approached and they were eventually towed to Limassol, Cyprus. Authorities on Cyprus described the deplorable conditions on the *Atlantic*. Besides overcrowding and absolute lack of any proper facilities extreme concern was expressed about the diseases. Outbreaks of typhoid and other illnesses soon swept through the ship, debilitating the passengers even further.

The other two ships, the *Pacific* and *Milos*, continued their parallel journey to Palestine and reached it by the beginning of November. The British Colonial Office in charge of Palestinian affairs was monitoring the situation closely. The British on the surface at least expressed the usual concerns about enemy agents being on board the refugee ships. Bernard Wasserstein in his book *Britain and the Jews of Europe* quotes a British official as expressing the belief that they were going to experience "a danger to public security with the influx of groups of young toughs who may or may not be Jews but are sure to have enemy agents amongst them." It is questionable as to whether the British really believed the allegations of enemy agents hidden amongst Jewish refugees or if they were merely using the allegations as a scare tactic.

The British discussed deporting the refugees en masse to Australia. Then it was realized that Mauritius, a tropical island in the Indian Ocean, was a more feasible destination. A telegram was sent to the governor of Mauritius asking him to provide accommodations for approximately four thousand refugees. It was stipulated by the governor that the Jewish refugees would have to be kept in a guarded camp surrounded with barbed wire.

When Winston Churchill heard of this and other similar plans to intern Jewish refugees in settings similar to those of a concentration camp, he protested vehemently. These types of plans, whether at Mauritius, Cyprus, or the camp in Palestine, Atlit, were all deplored by Churchill. Unfortunately far too often his protests were lost in the tumult of war and its aftermath, as well as in the vast bureaucracy of the British civil service. For the most part, Jews who were interned by the British were kept in concentration-camp-type internment facilities, comprised of barbed wire, stockades, searchlights, armed guards with dogs, and watchtowers. Most Holocaust survivors commented that these camps differed little from the Nazi camps, except that no one was being starved to death, worked to death, or murdered.

The governor of Mauritius agreed to accept the four thousand Jews provided that they bought their own bedding and tableware and sufficient guards, doctors, and interpreters were provided. Many of these Jews were of German, Polish, and Czech origins. In a final burst of stipulations, the governor ordered that chamber pots be provided and all refugees be vaccinated and fumigated. Considering that it was the fall of 1940, it is hard to conceive that so much detail and planning could go into placing a few thousand Jewish refugees. France had fallen in May, and Britain was alone in the world and facing a victorious German war machine. To simply admit these wretched people into Palestine would have been a far simpler solution; however, the British were obsessed with the fate of European Jewry. They simply were not going to allow them into Palestine.

The *Milos* and *Pacific* had been intercepted by British patrol ships when they arrived in Haifa. All of the passengers were held on the two ships in deplorable conditions while moored in the harbour. The British had made their decision and were going to deport the three shiploads of approximately four thousand refugees that were fleeing for their lives from the Nazi terror all the way to Mauritius.

After the fall of France, the British had seized from the Vichy government a French passenger liner named the *Patria*. The *Patria* was a 12,000-ton ship, twenty-seven years old, and required a crew of 130 hands. As a passenger liner it had been permitted to carry only eight hundred people, including the crew. The British had converted it to a troop carrier, raising its maximum occupancy to 1,800 soldiers. It had sufficient lifeboats for only the original occupancy limit of eight hundred passengers. Being twenty-seven years old, the steel hulled ship had a lot of wear and tear, and many rivets in the hull were loose.

Soon the passengers of the *Milos* and *Pacific* were transferred to the aged and decrepit *Patria*. The British awaited the arrival of the *Atlantic* passengers and prepared to imprison them on the *Patria*. The Jewish world, whether in North America or in Palestine, watched with horror as this deportation proceeded. A national strike was called and observed by the Jews in Palestine on November 20, 1940. Energetic protests against the British actions spread across many Jewish communities, but to no avail. A war was going on, and it was easy to divert attention from these deplorable actions. Numerous Zionist organizations met to consider alternatives. Even the Mapai party, the labour Zionists, were split on how to react. The active faction of Mapai, the Haganah, decided on a severe action. The Irgun, the militant force of the right-wing Revisionists, had already unsuccessfully attempted to place a bomb onboard the *Patria* with the intention of disabling the ship and forcing it to remain in port for repairs, thus forestalling the deportations. Finally in a second attempt a 2 kilogram bomb was smuggled aboard by the Haganah and placed near the inner hull. The passengers of the *Atlantic*, which was in dock, had not yet been transferred to the *Patria*.

On the morning of November 25 a tremendous explosion ripped through the inner hull of the *Patria*. The aged ship's hull, with its many loose rivets, simply blew apart. In addition the Haganah had miscalculated and far too much explosive material had been used. The ship almost immediately capsized, drowning many of the passengers, who were trapped down below in the dark hold. In vain, many small boats, both Arab and Jewish, circled the harbour picking up survivors. The final death toll was well over 250 people.

The British Colonial Administration announced with regret that there was a serious explosion on board the illegal refugee ship the *Patria*.

It further explained in its bulletin that the 1,800 illegal immigrants were about to be sent to an unnamed British colony. Most of the passengers were saved by scrambling onto the pier before the ship capsized and sank. The Palestine Council of Hadassah rushed six large cases of warm clothing to Haifa in order to comfort the survivors.

It was never clear until years later who was responsible for this terrible disaster. While the actual explosion was definitely caused by the Haganah, the British Mandate authorities must share some of the blame. To deport several thousand pitiful refugees fleeing from Nazi Germany to a faraway tropical island at this juncture in the war was a terrible deed. In 1957, Manya Mardor, a Haganah operative, wrote a book in which he assumed responsibility for the blast.

After the disaster, many pleas were made to the British authorities to accept the remaining refugees into Palestine. Finally a tiny bit of sympathy was shown by the British. It was decided that all those on board the *Patria* who had survived the blast and capsizing would be allowed into Palestine. Passengers from the *Patria* were sent to Atlit along with the passengers of the *Atlantic*, who had never boarded the *Patria*. The two groups were kept completely separate, as it was decided to deport the *Atlantic* passengers to the original destination of Mauritius.

At the almost exact same time, in November 1940, another far more catastrophic event for the Jewish people was taking place in Warsaw, as 400,000 Jews of the city were imprisoned in a ghetto about 2 square miles in size. An additional 100,000 Jewish refugees from outlying areas were forced into the ghetto. The now 500,000 Jews of Warsaw did not have a single blade of grass, a tree, or even a bird to comfort them in their inhuman prison. The German authorities in Poland justified their actions in sealing the Jews into the ghetto by stating that it was necessary to prevent the spread of disease. At almost the same time as the *Patria* crisis, the *Palestine Post* printed a report about the Jews of Warsaw. The German propaganda dispatches were reprinted in the *Palestine Post*, an uncensored newspaper without any dissenting comment. This again shows how difficult it was for anyone to comprehend the horrors of the impending Holocaust.

Those *Atlantic* passengers who had not been loaded onto the *Patria* were now sequestered separately from the survivors of the *Patria* disaster. The many protests from America and the Jews of Yishuv had probably steeled the will of the British officials. They began to plan to assemble and then deport the *Atlantic* passengers to Mauritius. Moshe Shertok, the head of the political department of the Jewish Agency, met with the British High Commissioner to plead the case of the surviving refugees. The meeting ended with an acrimonious exchange and the commissioner said in response to Shertok's arguments "that sometimes governments have to face unpleasant situations."[6] In addition, another British official commented, "The Jews have no sense of humour and no sense of proportion."[7] Despite all the arguments and protests, the deportations of the *Atlantic* passengers proceeded.

On December 9 the Atlit camp was surrounded by both army and police units. Many military vehicles were brought in and the British made sure everyone realized that a huge show of force was being made to frighten the immigrants. Nevertheless the refugees decided to resist. No one would pack their belongings, as few as they were, and everyone removed all their clothing. The migrants, young and old, male and female, lay naked on their beds as the British entered. The British forces in Palestine were renowned for their proper military dress, comprised of well-pressed khaki shorts with knee-high socks and khaki shirts with the appropriate insignia. It must have been quite a contrast between the neat British soldiers and their naked antagonists. The soldiers carried clubs and sticks to prod and beat the migrants. While no one was seriously hurt, many were beaten. The refugees were carried one by one on stretchers and blankets to the waiting trucks. One immigrant had no clothes and carried only his violin. Old men fell on the ground and kissed it. Many cried and pleaded with the impassive polices officers. Some of these people, particularly the German Jews, had already passed through Buchenwald and Dachau. All their protests were in vain.

---

6   Bernard Wasserstein.
7   Ibid.

While some British officers probably revelled in the clubbing and use of force, others grew pale and simply left. Certainly not every British officer and soldier was anti-Semitic or wanted to engage in such tactics. Eventually all the immigrants were forced onto trucks and the convoy proceeded to the port. The Inspector-General of the police denied allegations of police brutality but conceded that there had been considerable resistance and that the operation had been "a distasteful task."

Amongst the weary refugees were over six hundred women and one hundred children. As a final insult, a customs examination confiscated many personal articles, some of considerable value, including cameras, razors, jewellery, watches, and even tin mugs. Disputes about the monetary value of the confiscated items dragged on for several years, until the British authorities realized the extent of the public relations disaster. It rankled the refugees that the articles taken from them were sold at auction. Many of the objects were highly personal in nature and of considerable value to the distraught immigrants. Final payments were not made to the remaining imprisoned refugees until April 1945.

Many of the refugees lost their lives in transit to Mauritius. Typhoid had been detected on the *Atlantic* prior to the docking in Cyprus and subsequently in Haifa. Typhoid raged through the ship in transit to Mauritius and then when they docked on the tropical island. More than forty of the migrants died from disease while on the way to the island or immediately after their arrival.

Despite protests from the Czech government in exile, numerous Jewish organizations, and even the German government, which had not realised the Jewish origins of the internees, some 1,500 Jews were ultimately detained on Mauritius for several years. In 1945, when the war had ended, the perpetual exclusion ban for Palestine was finally lifted for the Jews of Mauritius. Over 80 percent chose to leave their tropical exile and migrate to Palestine.

The Patria before sinking in the Haifa harbour.

CHAPTER 5

Journey to Mauritius

The British Government and Colonial Administration were obsessed with keeping the Jews out of Palestine. In order to keep them out and deny them entry to the Promised Land, a strong British blockade was maintained from the time of the Arab revolt in 1935 until the British relinquished their mandate in May 1948. The question for the British became what to do with those detained. The detainees, desperate to escape Nazi-controlled Europe, were sent to Cyprus, Mauritius, or Atlit, a British-controlled concentration camp in Palestine. In the immediate postwar years some hardliners were sent to Eritrea near Somalia in East Africa.

In 1946, a certain Yitzhak Yezernitsky was arrested by the British Mandate authorities. Yezernitsky had become a thorn in the side of the British. He had been involved with both the Lehi and the Stern gang, both extreme right-wing organizations. Following the July 1946 bombing of the King David Hotel in Jerusalem Yezernitsky was detained and sent to Eritrea, which many dubbed Britain's Guantanamo Bay. There he spent months in a stifling tropical climate. Despite all the guards, barbed wire, and British precautions, Yezernitsky escaped, smuggled out in a water barrel tank. This short, tough little man made his way, disguised, to a French African colonial possession, Djibouti near Somalia. From there he took refuge in Paris, eventually arriving in Israel after independence in May 1948.

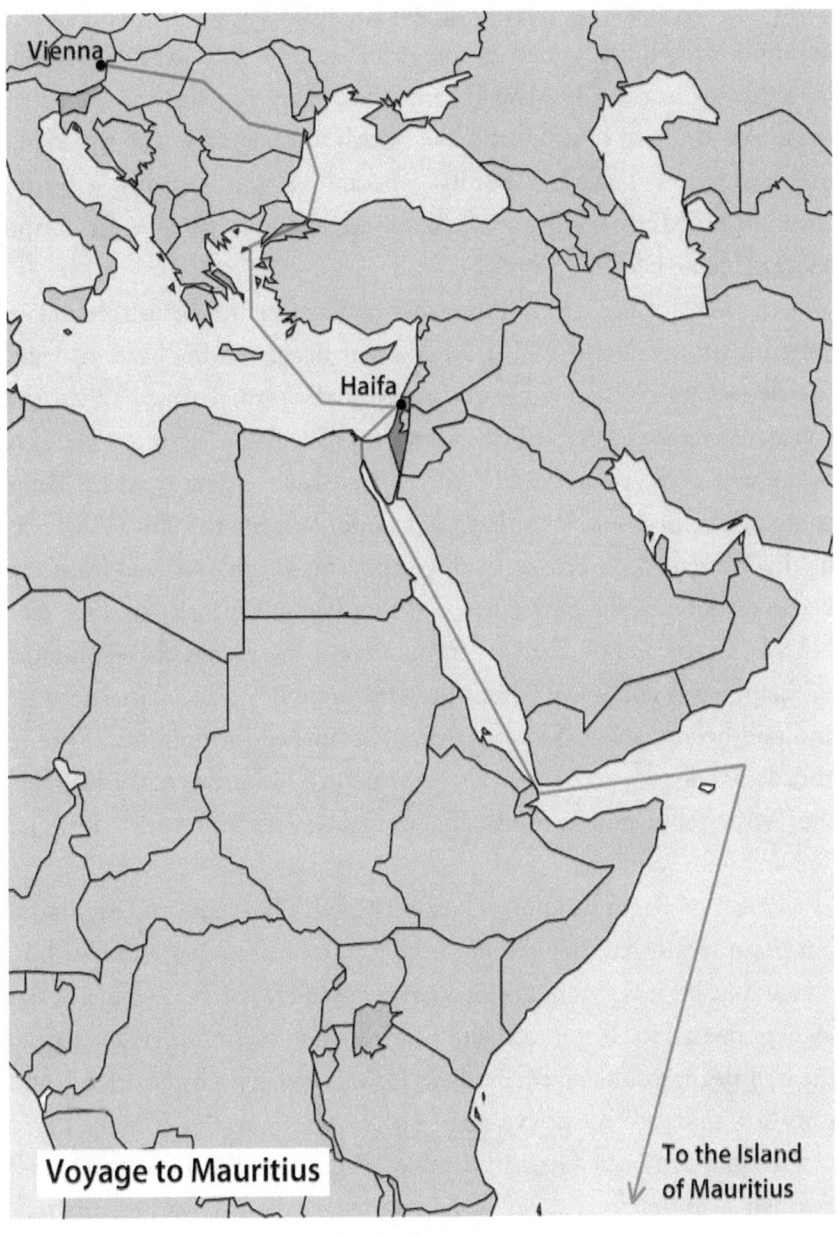

Voyage to Mauritius

To the Island
of Mauritius

Island of Mauritius

Yitzhak Yezernitsky, who had come to Palestine from Poland in 1935, had a strong grudge against the British. There was never enough money for the costly British immigration certificates for his parents, both of whom subsequently died in the Holocaust. Yitzhak, besides possible involvement in the King David Hotel bombing, was also connected to the assassination of Lord Moyne, the British administrator who was killed in Cairo. Later Yitzhak Yezernitsky became Yitzhak Shamir, a future Israeli Prime Minister. Shamir was involved for almost twenty years in the Mossad before becoming a politician.

Another future Israeli Prime Minister came to British Mandate Palestine during World War II. Menachem Begin was the head of Betar, the right-wing revisionist's youth group in Warsaw, Poland. When the Germans attacked Poland in September 1939, Begin agonized for days as the Germans approached. Finally, after strong urging from his Betar compatriots, Begin took the last train out of Warsaw to Vilna. Vilna was in the Russian occupied zone of Poland and Begin was safe from the Nazis. As soon as the Soviets realized that Begin was in Vilna, they sent NKVD, the secret police, to arrest him. Begin, aware that the communist "Gestapo" was coming for him, dressed properly with a shirt and a tie and polished his shoes. Suitably attired, he opened the door to the police and demanded an arrest warrant. Apparently his father had befuddled the Tsarist secret police, the Okhrana, many years before with a similar demand for a warrant.

This time Begin was not so lucky. The NKVD agents told him in no uncertain terms that they did not need a warrant for a Jew and beat him mercilessly. He was sent to the Siberian gulag and found himself in a brutal logging operation. If not for help from Revisionist Zionist sympathizers, the frail Begin would have soon died. He was kept alive by his friends and somehow managed to survive.

In June 1941, the Germans invaded Russia and the Soviets staggered through a horrendous series of defeats. They decided to get aid from wherever and whomever they could. General Anders of the Polish Free Army was liberated from Soviet imprisonment and allowed to continue the fight against the Germans. Menachem Begin was an officer in the

Polish army and was allowed to rejoin Anders' army. Somehow Begin made his way from the Siberian gulag by rail and by foot to Iran and from Iran to Palestine. In typical Begin fashion, he insisted on being properly discharged from the Polish army rather than being accused of desertion. After his epic journey to Palestine, Begin assumed command of the Irgun, the right-wing revisionist army, and began to terrorize the British. Two remarkable men, Yitzhak Shamir and Menachem Begin, who both became future prime ministers of Israel, had unbelievable journeys from exile to join the struggle against the British Mandate.

Karl Lenk was a Viennese Jew who decided to flee Austria after the 1938 Anschluss and, together with others, embarked on a perilous journey to seek illegal immigration to Palestine. A friend of Lenk, Dr. Edel, had also left Vienna on a Danube steamer called the *Uranus*, which subsequently became ice bound in the river. The *Uranus* got as far as Klavado, where the passengers were disembarked and eventually murdered by the Nazis.

Lenk made his way from Vienna to Bratislava, which was then in Czechoslovakia. There he boarded a steamer that travelled the Danube, called the *Helios*. This was a sister ship to the *Uranus*. The Danube steamship line owned a "fleet" of such ships which plied the Danube taking people on pleasure cruises. Lenk described the horrendous conditions on boarding the *Helios*. Slovakian guards brutally beat and punched them while looting their luggage. The distraught passengers called themselves by their city of origin, so there were Praugers, Berliners, and Danzigers. As in any situation, the first to arrive were not anxious to share their accommodations with the later arrivals. In the tumult of boarding, one man trying to safeguard his wife and child was knocked off of the gangplank and drowned. The *Helios* finally sailed from Bratislava on September 3, 1940.

The Praugers soon established a police force, the "Haganah," modelled after the Haganah in Palestine, to keep internal order. The crew was comprised of Austrians and Germans, many of whom were anxious but happy to leave their fatherland. Conditions on the ship were deplorable as people put down their bedding wherever they could, including gangways, decks, and floors. There were 1095 men, women and children on board the *Helios*. The "Haganah" guards were posted at the drinking water taps, the inadequate toilet facilities and the food line-ups.

When they arrived in the Bulgarian port of Varna, they met a dirty grey paddle steamer called the *Pencho*. This decrepit ship contained three hundred haggard looking Slovakian Zionists. The *Pencho* had almost no food and the beleaguered passengers all looked emaciated. They lined the decks, begging for food. The *Helios*, as well as two other Danube steamers, passed food and money to the passengers of the *Pencho*, who were all Betar[8] members and somehow managed to survive their ordeal. Eventually the *Pencho* moved through to the Black Sea, then the Bosphorus, and into the Mediterranean Sea, where it floundered at the island of Rhodes. In the end, the *Pencho*'s passengers somehow managed to arrive in Palestine.

The *Helios* pressed on and finally reached the Black Sea at the Romanian port of Tulcea. The passengers of the *Helios*, as well as the other refugee ships, boarded three ancient semi-derelict vessels, the *Atlantic*, the *Pacific*, and the *Milos*. They were all Greek vessels being refitted for their voyage to Palestine. The ships all bore Panamanian flags, and the passengers for the most part had exit visas to Paraguay. Karl Lenk boarded the *Atlantic*. Lenk described the passage as a living hell. Nineteen hundred people were jammed into a ship which barely had room for twelve hundred. This flotilla began to prepare to sail on September 14, 1940.

Conditions on board the *Atlantic* were appalling. Sleeping passengers and luggage choked every bit of space. The ventilation and light shafts were filled with clothing, overcoats, and luggage, which blocked off all light and air. When people who were sleeping on the deck climbed down into the hold, known as the catacombs, they were so repelled by the crowding and stench that they soon resumed their places on deck.

These ships were always at the mercy of profiteers who adulterated the food, made bread with low grade flour, and sold them spoiled meat. Soon people were sick from the mouldy bread and rotten meat. Cramps and dysentery became the rule. As well, lice, which eventually caused typhoid,

---

[8]   Revisionist youth group.

became endemic throughout the *Atlantic*. Some of the Orthodox prevailed and subsisted on their prepared kosher food. The Praguers continued to keep discipline, and several who had previous experience provided leadership. Those that were knowledgeable supplied proper cooking utensils, emergency lighting, buckets, brooms, and ropes. The voyage to Palestine was to last ten days but eventually went on for ten long weeks.

Several people, unable to take the stress, committed suicide. The captain deserted and had to be forced back on board. People were sleeping in the few lifeboats and others were trying to sleep standing up. Life jackets were used as pillows. Finally, on October 6, 1940, after four weeks of preparation, the ship's engines were lit and the *Atlantic* was underway. The luggage and the poor distribution of the passengers constantly caused the ship to list. Whistles were constantly being blown to move passengers from side to side. Still, the passengers, these stalwart refugees, had hope. Rosh Hashana came and the entire group of nineteen hundred passengers shouted in unison "next year in Jerusalem."

On October 7, only the second day of the journey, the ship ran aground. Someone checked the wording on the engine plates, which was in English. The ship had been commissioned in the 1870s and was more than seventy years old. The ship was towed free and then a proper pilot was found to navigate them into the Black Sea. Fights broke out between passengers and whistles were blown to separate combatants. It was carefully observed that the Black Sea was really black because of its depth and extreme cold.

Soon they reached the Bosphorus and watched both continents, Asia and Europe, in the distance. Elegant cafés and resort hotels lined the shores as crowds of Turkish spectators stood on lit terraces. The *Atlantic*'s passengers, crowded into their cramped quarters, could hear dance music.

Yom Kippur came on the eleventh of October. Some fasted because of religious observance, others because of lack of food. Turkish police came on board just before they entered the Aegean Sea. The Turks admonished everyone one last time that no one was allowed to enter into Turkey. They were running out of coal for the engine, and the devious captain was looking for ways to further swindle the refugee passengers. To compound their problems, the eastern Mediterranean was awash with naval vessels from several navies looking for targets. German, British, and Italian ships were all patrolling the area. Two storms hit the *Atlantic*, tossing the ship around like a toy in a bathtub. Everyone was seasick, and most were drenched with both sweat and seawater.

Finally they arrived in Heraklion, Crete. A refugee committee, headed by a Mr. Sevila from the Joint, appealed to the Greek-Jewish community for money, coal, and food provisions. Another woman died. Fresh drinking water and some mouldy bread arrived as well as wine, eggs, and butter. The coal arrived from Greece and the *Atlantic* was underway again.

Life on board the ship was dominated by line-ups. The pitiful passengers lined up for tea, for water, for bread, for soup, for the doctor, and for the dispensary. Above all, they lined up for the wretched toilet facilities. No one was allowed ashore or even near a pier when they docked, as word had spread that the ship was full of typhoid. More coal was loaded aboard on November 5 and the ship carried on. At the same time the captain was kept under guard by the "Haganah." The passengers were terrified that the captain would desert them or steal their possessions and supplies. Two stalwart young men guarded the captain at all times, and sentries were posted at the engines, coal bunkers, and food stores. Finally the captain asked for clemency and to return to duty with his crew. They were at sea and could hear naval bombardment in the distance. The passengers in charge relented and the captain resumed command.

Because of the acute shortage of coal they all decided to use any wood on the ship as fuel. Axes began to hack away at the superstructure of the ship, chopping at the bunks, the partitions, doors, cabin walls, and floors. All of this wood was fed into the furnace and kept the fires burning, the steam coming and the ship moving.

Soon two war ships appeared on the horizon. Engines were immediately shut down, and the *Atlantic* drifted. The passengers and crew all panicked as they awaited bombardment from the two vessels. Light signals were flashed, and they all soon realized that the ships were British. The *Atlantic* pleaded for food, water, and fuel. As dusk approached the two ships turned and were soon swallowed by the darkness. Before they left the British promised to send aid.

The cannibalisation of the ship continued as everything wooden was torn apart and fed to the boiler to raise steam. The weather was fine and the sea was calm, providing something of a respite for the weary crew and passengers. As the *Atlantic* limped along, a continuous stream of SOS signals was sent out pleading for help. The ship came to a dead stop and the engines ceased; there was no more fuel. A British motor launch approached and told them that they were close to Cyprus. Soon a tugboat towed them to Limassol, a city on the southern coast of Cyprus. They were at the end of their rope. As Karl Lenk put it, there was no more wood for the engine, only a few pieces of mouldy bread, and barely enough water to brew a cup of tea.

On November 14, the bargaining began for food and fuel. Everyone's valuables, including their personal jewellery and wedding rings, were seized to barter for the precious provisions. The "Haganah" searched all the luggage to ensure that everyone contributed. An upright piano which had been overlooked in the wood chopping frenzy was exchanged for coal. All of the foreign currency from the disparate group of Poles, Austrians, and Czechs was put into the community pot. By November 16 the equivalent of 500£ had been raised. Oranges were given to the children. Still more died from the malnutrition, stress, and exhaustion.

By November 17, 1940, the Cypriot press began to write about the beleaguered *Atlantic*.[9] They wrote about the hunger, the thirst, the dismemberment of the ship, and the horrible conditions. As a result of the sympathetic press, a lot of compassion was generated for the fifteen hundred refugees and their difficult lot. Soon oranges, grapefruits, potatoes, butter, raisins, and syrup all found their way to the ship. Then food that the hungry passengers had forgotten even existed began to arrive—eggs, white flour, corned beef, sardines, coffee, and even cocoa. They all began to eat two and three healthy meals a day for the first time in several months.

---

[9]   At this point the British had not yet interned any Jewish refugees on Cyprus.

A British officer and platoon of soldiers arrived to accompany them on the last leg of their journey from Cyprus to Haifa in the Promised Land. People began to sing and attempted to dance despite the crowded space. They all began to forget the horrors that they had faced for so many months. Soon, as the sun came up, Mt. Carmel loomed up overlooking Haifa. They saw Haifa as a large and modern city, bright and clean in the distance. As they moved themselves just outside of the harbour they saw their two sister ships, the *Milos* and the *Pacific*. But both ships appeared to be deserted. Two large ferryboats arrived and under heavy police guard the passengers began to disembark. Everything they had was subjected to careful inspection. All documents, books, newspapers, and letters were seized. All luggage was searched and taken off separately.

Disturbing rumours began to circulate. A large grey passenger liner, the *Patria*, stood in the distance. The rumours they heard startled everyone. They all stood in disbelief. After this incredible journey could it be true that they were going to be deported to Mauritius, an island in the Indian Ocean east of Madagascar? No one could believe that after the ordeal they had been through, the British were going to banish them to this faraway island. Slowly groups of the passengers, mainly women, children, and families, were ferried to the landside, from where they would be transferred to the *Patria*. Suddenly there was a large explosion, after which Lenk described the *Patria* sinking.

The next morning, November 28, 1940, the rest of the *Atlantic* passengers were taken ashore and interned in Atlit, the British concentration camp in Palestine. The refugees were happy to stand on dry land but were not happy with the rough treatment. Many people had lice and all were fumigated on their bus ride to internment at Atlit. All were overwhelmed with the cleanliness and order of Jewish Palestine. The food at the camp was excellent, especially considering the deprivations and near starvation they had been through. Once they got to the actual detention centre at Atlit they realized that the camp at Akko was much cleaner and better organized.

On December 8 Karl Lenk described the official announcement that all those passengers who had survived the *Patria* and had been on board would be allowed to stay, while the rest of the refugees who had not been in the *Patria* would be deported to Mauritius. Lenk recalled the traditional right of asylum that the British were always so proud of. Where was it?

As Karl Lenk left Palestine, a forlorn man destined to be exiled to faraway Mauritius, he described the confiscation of most of the personal items of the detainees. All cameras, watches, razors, metal plates, mess tins, cooking utensils, and cutlery were seized. Underwear, food, medicine, bottles, cigarettes, and even toilet articles were also taken. Women who had been on the *Patria* and survived the sinking were allowed to stay in Palestine, while their husbands, who had never made it to the *Patria*, were going to be deported. Anyone who protested was roughly handled, and many were searched two or three times.

Karl Lenk's last comments about the painful exile process ring true. The Jews were but pawns in the imperial game that the British were playing in Palestine. They had forgotten the Balfour Declaration and that these were refugees fleeing Hitler and Nazi Germany. They had forgotten that the Grand Mufti of Jerusalem Husseini was in Berlin broadcasting Nazi propaganda. They had forgotten that most Arabs supported the Germans and were waiting for Rommel's victories. They had forgotten the civility and good manners of Britain. Their policy was a bankrupt one that would not serve His Majesty's Government well.

The deportees were shunted back to the port and found themselves boarding a Dutch East Indian ship called the *New Zealand* (*Nieuw Zeeland*). Unlike the *Atlantic*, the ship, which had been converted to a troop carrier, seemed spacious, clean, and well lit. It was airy and well ventilated. The passengers had rooms with tables and chairs, and they even had hammocks in which to sleep. But the ship was guarded with armed policemen who could be rough and hostile. There was a sister ship called the *Johan de Wit*. Again and again Lenk emphasized that the Dutch officers were kind and sympathetic, in contrast to the cruel British.

Lenk also commented on the food, which was excellent. This preoccupation with food is certainly understandable given their three months of deprivation. The cleanliness of the former Dutch ship also seemed almost incomprehensible to Lenk. The two passenger ships had an escort of two British naval vessels, one in front and one behind. At the low point of Britain during the war it seems almost incomprehensible for the British to send four ships to deport fifteen hundred Jewish refugees to Mauritius, Jews that were on the British side, unlike the Arabs in Palestine. The typhoid that had dogged them on the *Atlantic* continued on the *New Zealand*, and several people died. Finally on December 27, 1940, the mountains of Mauritius come into view as they approached St. Louis, the capital.

They were moored in the harbour for three days until the arrangements were finalized. They were taken by bus through beautiful countryside to a jail. The cells were about ten feet high and quite sparse except for a hammock. There was a one-foot-square ventilation hole at the top covered by a wooden shutter. Mosquitoes, which eventually produced malaria, infested the entire area, and the British did not provide any mosquito nets for several weeks. The food was poor and very inconsistent both in quality and quantity. Typhoid that had been brought from the *Atlantic* was endemic. Between the malaria and the typhoid, almost fifty people died within the first month. Finally the confiscated luggage arrived in Mauritius, but to the surprise of no one, the locks had been forced and the contents had been looted. Most people only received a small sampling of the remnants of their personal items.

Lenk was never a well man and his bouts of malaria, dysentery, and probably typhoid depleted his reserves of health. He lived only to the age of fifty-nine, hoping beyond hope that he would one day be liberated from his tropical prison and be able to go to Palestine.

Henry Wellisch described the chaos following the Anschluss of Austria by the Germans in March 1938. Henry was told in September 1939 that he was subject to deportation to Poland. The Wellisch family decided that they would avoid the exile to Poland at all costs and found an illegal transport to Palestine. Apparently, with the consent of the German authorities and after paying some monies to a Zionist organization, they were able to proceed to Bratislava (Now in Slovakia).

Here the Wellisch family found themselves with hundreds of Czechoslovakian and Viennese Jews in a camp called Pressburg. It was

December 1939, and severe winter conditions caused the Danube to freeze. They were therefore forced to stay in Pressburg and were unable to embark until September 1940.

Finally Jewish organizations had made arrangements with the Danube steamship company, and some 3500 Jews sailed on four steamers down the river. After a week the flotilla reached the Danube delta and the Romanian port of Tulcea. Here they were transferred onto the three ships that have been mentioned, the *Atlantic*, the *Pacific*, and the *Milos*.

Henry's description of the appalling conditions on the *Atlantic* matches those of other passengers. As a result of the severe overcrowding, the ship listed badly and passengers were driven from one side to the other by the "Haganah." Several people died and were buried at sea.

As Lenk described it, the Greek captain was arrested and the ship ran out of coal. As a result all possible wood was stripped, chopped up, and used as fuel. Finally the *Atlantic* arrived in Haifa harbour. A few of the passengers were immediately transferred to the *Patria*, but following the explosion and capsizing, the rest were taken and sent to Atlit, where they were segregated from the other passengers that had been on the *Milos* and the *Pacific*.

Eventually Henry and his parents were disembarked on the two former Dutch ships, the *New Zealand* and the *Johan de Witt*. Unfortunately Henry was separated from his parents as he was placed on one ship and they on another. After an uneventful voyage that took then through the Suez Canal, the Red Sea, and the Indian Ocean, they arrived at Port St. Louis in Mauritius.

CHAPTER 6

Mauritius

The volcanic island of Mauritius.

During the war many thousands of Czech and Austrian Jews, such as Karl Lenk and Henry Wellisch, journeyed from the banks of the Danube River to the shores of Palestine. Another such person was Dr. Aaron Zwegerbaum, a Czechoslovakian Jew. In September 1940, he sailed with his family in the *Helios* to Constanza. There he boarded the *Atlantic* along with Karl Lenk. Like Lenk, in late 1940 Zwegerbaum was deported to Mauritius, where he remained for three years. Zwegerbaum's account of the detainee camp in Mauritius corroborates Lenk's account. There were about fifteen hundred Jews, most of them assimilated Czech, German, and Austrian middle-class people. They were kept at a prison called Beau Bassin, located about ten kilometres from St. Louis, the capital of Mauritius. The Jewish prisoners arrived on December 27, 1940, [10] and were separated by sex. The men were kept in the fort, which was surrounded by a massive stone wall, while the women had barracks of corrugated iron built for them.

As Zwegerbaum described it, the complex was not too bad considering it was a prison. When the prison gates were closed for the first time they all felt that it was more than an unpleasant surprise. The doctor had thought that from the outside it looked somewhat acceptable, but inside it resembled a decrepit railroad station. Bars were on all the windows, which had no glass. They had simple mats on which to sleep and virtually no other furnishings. They were grouped into sections of four or more persons. Some of the elderly people were happy to not be alone at night. While there seemed to be amply air and light, it was definitely a prison. After their experiences at sea in the various crowded refugee ships, the washing and toilet facilities were a welcome change.

Zwegerbaum went on to describe flower beds and lawns with various workshops and storerooms comprising the rest of the camp. Zwegerbaum went to great lengths to emphasize the strict separation of men and women. There was a connecting gate patrolled by an armed guard. No one was allowed to cross the gate without an escort or written permit. It seemed the British thought that they were dealing with criminals or perhaps the proverbial Nazi agents rather than refugees escaping from the clutches of the Holocaust.

The Jewish settlement on Mauritius comprised some 1580 people, including 849 men, 635 women, and 96 children. A number of people died from the typhoid that was endemic on the original ship, the *Atlantic*. After a year they had a net loss of some fifty people, including four births. Of the approximately 1500 people in the camp there were some 600 Austrians, 300 Poles, and 300 Czechoslovakians. They were additionally segregated by nationality, with people from Vienna separated from those from Danzig or Prague.

In any prison camp food becomes a major issue, but for most it became paramount. As most of these people were at least middle class, they were

---

[10]   The *Patria* bombing had occurred in November 1940.

used to far better food than the meagre rations that they received. As Zwegerbaum emphasized, no one starved, and compared to the ghettos of Europe it was extremely beautiful. Twice a week they lined up for three ounces of beef and three times a week six ounces of salmon. Bread, rice, a little margarine, and some fruit comprised most of the remainder of their paltry diet. Almost everyone soon lost weight. After the food was cooked, the result seemed to vary, but it was mostly bad.

Some clothing and shoes were distributed, but both the quality and quantity were completely insufficient. It should be borne in mind that most people came with almost nothing and that the British had confiscated most personal possessions and sold them off at public auction before they were deported from Palestine. During the first year the men received one pair of pants and a pair of poor shoes. One towel was also allotted. The women were luckier, as the South African Jewish community donated a large amount of women's clothing.

Zwegerbaum commented strongly on the lack of freedom and the inability to maintain any family life. Many of the inmates were very upset by the inability to have normal marital relationships. When men and women were allowed to see each other it was only in the open and under strict supervision. For men and women, regardless of whether they were married or not, cohabitation was strictly forbidden. This excessive Puritanism by the British authorities was to prevent children being born who could then claim Jewish-Mauritian nationality. As well one could also suspect the British were further punishing these Jewish refugees by denying them sex and determining that normal living was not part of the detainment process.

The British Home Minister and Colonial Administration also determined that there were to be no legal marriages countenanced on the island and that the six religious marriages that were performed were only ritually valid. Over three years of containment, only one child was born. In addition, Zwegerbaum described the strong police presence whenever couples met. This constant sexual separation and tyrannical supervision was found by all to be overbearing. Many felt that they were subjected to these strict conditions as punishment for defying the British Empire.

In addition to the sexual separation and deprivation, time passed very slowly. Anyone who has seen movies with people marking time on prison walls can imagine the tedium and boredom that the Jews of Mauritius felt. Men under fifty-five years of age were given obligatory work, but this was very sparse, menial, and mundane. The simple cleaning jobs that they were given left most of the day free for boredom. The artisans, comprised of tailors, shoemakers, plumbers, carpenters, bakers, and barbers were all paid for small tasks and given some work in the workshops. These people earned a few pounds sterling for their efforts and were able to buy little luxuries like chocolates and cigarettes. The so-called academic professionals, the medical doctors like Zwegerbaum, teachers, theologians, and other functionaries, received no money.

The elderly were bored to the point of psychosis. Some tried to learn English and practiced by reading newspapers. Interestingly French, which was the Mauritian language,[11] and Hebrew, the new language of Palestine, were largely ignored. Eventually most sat around and wiled away their time reading, gossiping, and playing cards. After a while they were allowed to listen to the radio, although this was sometimes censored. All tried to debate politics, but they were so isolated and confined that there was no real appreciation of the wartime situation.

Two organizations were formed: Zam, the Zionist Association of Mauritius, and a sports club, the Maccabees. Other than some delusory notes little was done about Zionist activity. The sports club consisted of many bystanders watching a few players. Gradually apathy set in as more and more people sat around waiting endlessly.

As in any Jewish settlement, there was a division over religion. Some formed themselves into an Orthodox community, while others called themselves a liberal Jewish community. There was a great concern about kosher meat from the Orthodox, who eagerly awaited the arrival of a large quantity of kosher salted meat from South Africa. After the meat arrived, an advertisement appeared in the community newspaper that

---

[11]   Mauritius was formerly a French colony that was captured from France in 1814 by the British during the Napoleonic wars.

dentures were available for lease on meat days. This of course referred to the apparent toughness of the meat.

In 1942, when the Nazi war machine was still predominant, the British authorities on Mauritius blocked BBC broadcasts in Polish and Czech. The reason given was that the war news was too bad and too depressing. This must have sent a stir through the interned on Mauritius.

Most detainees complained about their emotional depression. The terrible sense of confinement in a faraway and desolate place was devastating. Surrounded always by the four walls and all the rules and regulations, the inmates also worried about what had become of their relatives. Almost no one was able to find out anything concrete or specific. In addition to the British censorship, the Nazis had hermetically sealed German occupied Europe. There were vague rumours and speculations in 1940 and 1941 but no one really knew or could comprehend what was happening. Again it is important to state that the mass killing of Jews did not start until June 1941, when the Germans invaded Russia. The fifteen hundred Jews of Mauritius, mostly middle class and used to better things, were beset with their own physical problems as well as worries about the Jews still left in Europe.

The rumours that permeated the psyche of the internees were exacerbated by the geography. The people interned heard about occupied Europe, Palestine, and a Britain that was standing alone against the German war machine, as well as South Africa, Australia, Rhodesia, and an isolationist United States. The years 1940 and 1941 saw a series of unparalleled triumphs for Adolf Hitler. Many expressed concerns that Rommel would sweep across North Africa and invade the Jewish refuge of Palestine.

The cruelty of the British administration added to the woes of the prisoners. Most of their possessions had been confiscated in Haifa, leaving some virtually naked. As Zwegerbaum described it, soon money transfers began to arrive. People from South Africa and other places abroad sent money to aid the refugees. The British decided to impose an excise tax of 5 percent on all money transfers to help fund the camp. This generated fierce controversy amongst the inmates. Many felt that they would not participate in the so-called obligatory work. A virtual strike ensued.

Still others produced items for sale to help generate revenue. Thirty people were involved in making toys, which were sold throughout Mauritius. Some of the chemists among the prisoners produced marmalade, which was also sold as a delicacy throughout the island.

Dr. Zwegerbaum concluded that the cultural activities were the one area that was satisfactory. Five hundred books from the local police library satisfied the English and French readers. In addition, the Jewish community in South Africa sent more than six hundred books in German for the detainees to read. A variety of Hebrew books, journals, and newspapers also kept the refugees busy. Zwegerbaum boasted that they had Jewish newspapers from four continents. As one might suspect in any Jewish community, an adult education centre was established. At first the centre was a big success, but interest gradually petered out. Most inmates of the Mauritius prison camp sank into a kind of depressed lethargy.

Some of the Mauritian Jewish inmates were able to speak and write English. As a result two British men, F. E. Ward, a director of education, and Mr. Otter-Bary, the Anglican bishop of Mauritius, came to offer various courses. Both these men were very busy and yet came to offer their skills to the Jewish inmates. In addition, the bishop organized a trip to the nearby sugar factory. This showed that some of the British officials were indeed very compassionate.

While the Jewish prisoners appreciated the concerns shown by some, there was constant censorship of mail. When the inmates weighed the mail they found what they had sent out was tremendously disproportionate to what was received.

Still Zwegerbaum emphasized the Zionist activities. The Jewish Mauritians honoured Herzl, Chaim Nahman Bialik, and Trumpeldor. Two important Zionist leaders died abroad during their internment, the US Supreme Court Justice Brandeis and the Russian-born Menachem Ussishkin. Both had commemoration ceremonies on Mauritius. Although all fifteen hundred internees were not Zionists, many became Zionists due to their terrible confinement. In the end, after the war almost all made the long journey to Palestine.

In 1942 Aaron Zwegerbaum described the conditions as somewhat improved. The deadly typhoid was gone, but there were still many cases of dysentery and malaria. The food was much better as meat was provided four times a week. The British restrictions on family life were still the most irritating aspect of camp life. It was observed that there were numerous decrees about sexual separation during air raid drills so as not to violate public morality.

Finally, in the summer of 1942, camp orders were issued allowing married couples to mingle. Subsequently some thirty couples were married. This lessening of social constraints did wonders for morale. In addition, the workshops became more productive and people began to earn a little money. The wages were very low, between 10 and 30 cents per day. Medical doctors received 40 cents per day, while advisors and supervisors received 30 cents per day. However, Zwegerbaum explained that prices in the camp were very low. Ten cents bought you a coffee with two rolls or ten cigarettes. Prices in Mauritius were also very low: 22 cents for a kilogram of sugar (about 2 pounds) and 40 cents for a litre of gas. Anything that was imported was much more expensive, especially clothing, shoes, and tinned goods. The lack of clothing was still a major issue, and most of the Mauritian Jews were still poorly clad in their second year of confinement.

Over and over Zwegerbaum emphasized the tremendous support they received from outside Jewish communities. The Orthodox Jewish community of South Africa sent food parcels and monetary donations. The Czechoslovakian Jews received donations from both South Africa and Palestine. In addition, several Palestinian *kibbutzim* sent aid. Realizing the situation of Palestine in 1942, strong letters were written to Palestine urging them to stop sending donations. The Jews of Mauritius realized their economic conditions and the lack of a threat of war made their situation better than that of the Palestinian Jews. Perhaps the most significant and uplifting news was that the Jewish Agency had applied to the British authorities for immigration certificates to Palestine. The British authorities refused the request, and the Jews of Mauritius continued to languish in their imprisonment.

On Rosh Hashanah 1942, many telegrams, letters, and cards arrived from London, South Africa, and Palestine. Those being held on Mauritius knew that they had not been forgotten. Then they received the long delayed news about the *Struma*. The death of almost all of the eight hundred passengers was a devastating blow to the imprisoned Jews. In addition, they also received news that numerous protests had been mounted on their behalf. Moshe Shertok, the future Israeli Foreign Minister, commented that Mauritius was Dachau for the Yishuv.

By 1943, 40 percent of all prisoners suffered from malaria, with many having complications of the liver and gall bladder as a result of the illness. Some 15 percent still suffered from dysentery, and a shocking 50 percent had severe vitamin deficiencies. A number of young people suffered heart attacks as more and more of the inmates went into melancholic depression. Zwegerbaum sarcastically noted that there was only one suicide.

In June 1943, the governor of Mauritius came to inspect the prison. This was preceded by a tremendous amount of preparation, which strongly irritated the Jews. Nothing came of the inspection visit. The pleas, petitions, private interventions, and parliamentary interventions all came to naught. The Jews stayed in Mauritius.

To placate the suffering inmates, they were allowed a sort of camp out on the northeast shore of the island. Tents were pitched and many enjoyed the fresh air. Suddenly everything changed. The main camp was occupied by military personnel. Everyone had to attend roll call in the middle of the night, and all communication with the outside world was cut off. No one was allowed to go to the seaside, movie theatres, or outside jobs. What prompted the security crackdown is still not clear almost seventy years later. The various outside Jewish aid organizations marked it down to simple anti-Semitism. Some ascribed this alert to the fact that several allied ships had been sunk near Mauritius.

Many Jews tried to leave the island, some by volunteering for their respective countries' armies. Some were told that there were "difficulties of sea transportation." The Jewish Mauritians felt that there really was simply bad faith on the behalf of the authorities. Telegrams were sent to the Refugee Conference in Bermuda, although it was strongly suspected that the telegrams never arrived.

Henry Wellisch described the prison that held the fifteen hundred Jewish passengers of the *Atlantic* as a miserable penal institute. He also described the typhoid and malaria that decimated the camp. More than fifty people died in the first month.

Henry learned a new trade on Mauritius: carpentry. He also experienced the incessant boredom and the bad food, although he retains a memory of eating Canadian salmon from tins. In addition to the British staff, the camp was guarded by numerous Mauritians. Despite the lazy guards and the non-secure prison, there were no attempts to escape confinement.

While the British guards obviously spoke English and the Mauritian guards spoke Creole, the language of the camp was mainly German. It should be emphasized that the Jewish inmates were a mixture of Austrians, Poles, Czechs, and others. Despite the polyglot Tower of Babel, a feature of the camp was the nightly BBC broadcasts in English at nine o'clock in the evening. Henry manned the radio room and used two loudspeakers to keep the camp up to date on the world situation. There are conflicting views on the amount of censorship that the British imposed. Henry also related that music was played extensively over the loudspeakers. He remembers that despite the language difficulties, jazz and Frank Sinatra were both very popular. A gramophone with vinyl records was also used to entertain the Jewish inmates.

While Henry also spoke about the incessant boredom the four long years were also marked by numerous activities, including the study of Greek and British history. It should be remembered that most of the prisoners were middle class people. Some of the Czechs Henry knew would have been considered upper class. Wellisch said, in addition, that most of the Czechs were Zionistic. However he found that amongst the Viennese there were quite a few communists. In particular Henry remembered one extremely dedicated communist who eventually made his way to Palestine after the war, found himself in a kibbutz, and then, in despair, committed suicide.

Henry finally left Mauritius in March 1945 just before the war ended. He went through the Suez Canal and arrived at the Jewish Brigade headquarters in Egypt and commenced training. He was transferred to Holland and Belgium, where he subsequently helped assist Jewish refugees in the Bricha movement. Finally, in August 1945, Henry Wellisch rejoined his parents in

Pardes Hannah, Palestine, before they took up residence in Haifa. Henry went on to serve in the IDF before eventually immigrating to Canada.

After the war when given the option more than 80 percent of the prisoners did eventually immigrate to Palestine. The cruel and unnecessary restrictions imposed on the fifteen hundred people isolated on a far away, malaria-ridden island clearly exemplified the lengths to which the British Colonial Administration was willing to go to prevent the Jews from reaching Palestine. Above all, it had to be emphasized that these were Jewish refugees fleeing from death in Nazi occupied Europe. Beyond simple anti-Semitism, one has a feeling that it was in a way a process that once set in motion was unstoppable. Two similar processes set in motion that could not be stopped were the Holocaust and the Soviet purges of the 1930s.

CHAPTER 7

The Tehran Children

On August 22, 1939, a little over a week before the Second World War began, an infamous pact was signed by two monsters, Hitler and Stalin. The Molotov-Ribbentrop Pact had also been called the "pact of the devils." This treaty between Russia and Germany made World War II immediately possible. Secret protocols of the pact divided Poland into two spheres. The eastern portion was to be controlled by Russia and the western portion was to be terrorized by the Germans.

Russia entered the war on September 17, 1939, trying hard not to assume the role of an invader. By September 17, the Germans had already conquered much of the territory that had been allotted them. Warsaw and the some 400,000 Jewish people in the German occupied zone lay as helpless victims for their cruel Nazi overlords.

Poland, prior to its independence in 1919, had suffered several invasions from both the Russians and the Germans, the last being the Russian Red Army's attack in 1920, which attempted to convert the new Polish republic into a Communist state. The Russians especially, considering the long Polish sojourn under Tsarist Empire, were considered as barbarians. In contrast, the Germans who had occupied most of Poland in World War I, were perceived as haughty and arrogant. However badly the Germans were viewed by the Poles and the Jews, the Russians were seen as worse.

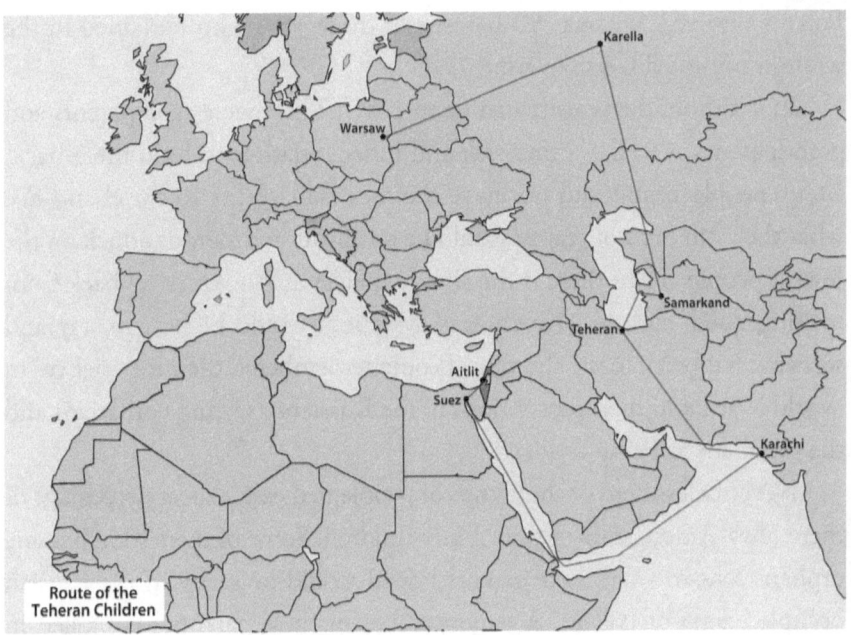

Voyage of the Tehran Children

An anecdote related by my father concerning the occupation of Warsaw in World War I reveals the arrogant, haughty attitude of Jewish officers in the German army. The officers were approached by the children of a Jewish family, my father among them, who lived near their army base and invited the Jewish officers to a Passover Seder. The Jewish officers in the Germany army thought that this was uproariously funny and laughed the little children away. This anecdote perhaps frames the view held by Polish Jews of the Germans as haughty and arrogant, but not murderous.

As the two powers, Germany and Russia, began to solidify their hold on Poland in September 1939, the border between them was still chaotic and uncontrolled. Thousands of people, Jews and non-Jews, began to flee. But which way where they to go? The apocryphal story is told of two trains jammed full of refugees passing each other, one going west and one going east. Most of the refugees on the trains were Jewish and yelled at each other that they were both going to certain death. In the end, some 90 percent of the Jews who were in the eastern Russian occupied zone of

Poland survived, whereas 90 percent of those Jews who remained in the western occupied German zone died.

In addition, many were unable to travel. There were aged parents and grandparents as well as other sick and infirm relatives to hold them back. Many people simply did not have the means or ability to travel and flee what they still did not realize would be an all-out murderous attack on the Jewish people. Then there is the simple inertia that holds us all back from making quick and decisive choices. Maybe it would be best to stay and see what happens, many thought. People remembered their experiences in World War I and their perceptions of the Russians as being barbarians and the Germans as being civilized.

Nevertheless, tens of thousands of people fled east, a great percentage of them Jews. Amongst them were many children. Some of them soon became orphans sent to what their parents hoped would be safety in the Russian occupied zone of Poland. A large number of these parents were killed in subsequent fighting or in the Holocaust that consumed Polish Jewry.

Men, women, and children who had fled to what appeared to be the safety of Russian occupied Poland were indeed safe, until June 22, 1941. On that day, 3.5 million German troops helped break their solemn pact with the Russians and invaded Russia and eastern Poland. The Russians hoped that their pact with the Germans would provide a buffer zone against future Nazi attacks. By the time of the invasion, most Jews were somewhat aware of the Germans' genocidal designs on them. The Nazis had established the first of their three phases concerning the eventual extermination of the Jews—identification, the wearing of the yellow star. The second phase, ghettoization and containment, had already been promulgated in German-occupied Poland in the fall of 1940. The third phase, extermination, was to begin shortly.

When the Wehrmacht, the regular German army, invaded Russia on June 22, they were followed by the *Einsatzgruppen*, mobile killing units that were specifically designated to kill Jews and Communist commissar officials. Word soon spread amongst the Jews of eastern Poland. Many were able to flee further east to avoid the Nazi onslaught. Amongst those fleeing were a group of more than one thousand children, mainly orphans, who later became known as the Tehran children.

Many of those who fled to the East and Russia from Poland were middle—and upper-class Jews. While most spoke at least some Polish, almost all spoke and read Yiddish. A favourite Yiddish newspaper of Warsaw that was popular throughout Poland was the *Haint*. Yiddish was their means of differentiating the Jews of Russia. The language had mainly died out in Communist Russia, but they still could find out if a person was Jewish by speaking a few words of their mother tongue, Yiddish.

The river Bug was the border between German and Russian occupied Poland. In the first weeks after the war began, it was largely uncontrolled and many thousands were able to escape to the east. Soon many of these terrified people found themselves exiled to northern Soviet slave labour camps. The Soviets especially targeted Zionist Jews. Logging, mining, and building were major occupations for the forced labourers. Quotas were given, and those who exceeded their quotas might be able to get a little food above the subsistence level. In the summer of 1941, following the German invasion, Soviet authorities decided to allow the Poles to form a Free Polish Army to fight the German invaders.

Prior to the German invasion in June 1941, relations between the Poles and the Russians had been very poor. Following the Nazi attack the Russians suffered a horrible series of unmitigated defeats. Following these horrendous losses, Russian authorities decided to set up a Polish army in exile to help them combat the Germans, thus creating a new alliance between the Russians and the Poles.

Many of the children that had fled east were orphans that were completely separated from their families. Chaos ruled, as people, children, and families were scattered across Russia. In addition to the deprivations of war, these poor people were dispersed across the length and breadth of an enormous country that spanned eleven time zones. Slowly the Polish authorities in Russian began to gather people together. An aid corridor was established for Russia and their newfound Polish allies in Iran. From there, western aid would flow through to Russia and help the war effort against the Germans. In addition, the Polish government, in exile, pleaded for many of the Polish civilians trapped in the war zone to be allowed to flee. As a result of all of these machinations, thousands of Polish Jews, amongst them the many Jewish orphans, were allowed to congregate in Persia (modern-day Iran).

The Jewish Agency in Palestine was well organised and on top of the situation. Slowly, in the spring of 1942, thousands of Polish Jewish citizens were assembled from the farthest reaches of the then Soviet Union. They came from Kazakhstan, from the Far East in Mongolia, and from across the length and breadth of the Soviet Union. The Jewish Agency assembled the Jewish children, most of them orphans, from the orphanages and shelters. The children travelled on trains and trucks to a Soviet assembly point called Krasnovodsk. From here, the children were sent by ship to an Iranian port called Pahlavi on the shores of the Caspian Sea. Others went via Bukhara to Kazan and Ashkhabad on the Iranian border before finally reaching the Iranian port of Pahlavi.

Soon the roads and trains were clogged with Polish and Jewish refugees trying to leave the Soviet Union. They could be transported to neutral countries and then be revitalized to fight the Nazis. The children in particular were in pitiful shape, suffering from endemic lice, the consequent typhoid, all manner of skin diseases, malnutrition, and eye infections. Nevertheless many thousands were able to get transport to the nearby neutral country of Persia. They found themselves at the port of Pahlavi on the Caspian Sea.

One can only imagine the culture shock of these Polish Jewish children in the Soviet oriental environment. For the most part they had no parents or family and were bereft of any Jewish connections. The Jewish Agency negotiated on behalf of the children with the Polish government in exile. Finally permission was granted and the children began to assemble in Tehran. There were numerous non-Jewish Polish children involved in this migration from all over Russia. The Jewish agency separated the Jewish and non-Jewish children; Polish authorities were to look after the gentile children. A major problem soon arose, as many of the Jewish children were so traumatized by their horrible experiences that they refused to acknowledge their Jewish identity.

Conditions were indescribably awful. It was summer and blazing hot. The children were half naked and barefoot. There were awful confrontations between the newly liberated Poles and their former Jewish neighbours. The endemic anti-Semitism that had previously marked Polish-Jewish relations too often continued in the refugee settings. Battles also commenced as many Polish priests wanted to take the opportunity to baptize and convert the young Jewish children.

There were quotas and immigration certificates to be concerned about, and so finally ways were found to establish the Jewishness of the children. The children were hungry, tattered, and dirty. The clothes that they wore looked like rags. The children ranged in age from one year old to eighteen years old, although most were between the ages of seven and twelve. Finally, when almost all the children were assembled in Tehran, the Zionist leaders David Ben-Gurion and Eliahu Dobkin began to negotiate with the British officials to get the precious immigration certificates to allow admission to Palestine.

Soon the Jewish Agency established a Jewish orphanage for the Tehran children. More than seven hundred of these children had arrived in Iran from April until August 1942. They lived in primitive tents in a former Iranian air force base just outside Tehran. More Polish-Jewish children continued to arrive in the summer of 1942. The camp acquired the name "The Tehranian Home for Jewish Children." It was supported by the local Iranian Jewish community, which was still very large, Hadassah, the Women's Zionist Organization in the United States, the American Jewish Joint Distribution Committee, and the Youth Immigration Department of the Jewish Agency. Everyone cried when they saw the poor, starving, threadbare children and support flowed in.

The Jewish Agency brought experienced Zionist leaders from Palestine to take charge of the Tehran Children's Orphanage. Many of the children were in terrible shape after enduring long periods of hardship. They were homeless and had been confined in terrible circumstances in makeshift shelters across Russia, which had been racked by a horrendous war. Many of the children were seriously ill, suffering from tuberculosis and malnutrition. Fortunately most of the children recovered their health in Tehran.

Many Palestinian Jews came from British Mandate Palestine to help the refugees. Over the first year of the Russo-German war, some 25,000 Polish refugees made their way to Pahlavi from Russia. Of these some 2,000 were Jewish, half of them being children aged mainly six to sixteen years. Many of the children, even those as young as six or seven, sold what was given to them in a sort of black market transaction. Blankets, shoes and clothing were all sold by the Jewish children in exchange for money. The orphan children also hoarded everything that they received. This is a common psychological response for those that have suffered the severe traumas of deprivation. Similar behaviour was seen in Holocaust survivors, who hoarded bread. The children's hoarding caused severe problems, as the excess food hidden in shoes and under beds usually became mouldy or attracted insects.

Another problem was that some of the children denied their Jewish origins. Some wore crosses and in addition were under tremendous pressure to convert to Catholicism from some of the Polish authorities. There were many rounds of tug-of-war over the young children. In several instances the Polish military police accused the Palestinian Jews of kidnapping Polish children. All of these scenes were heartbreaking, as everyone ended up crying. In addition, there were tearful reunions as parents were connected with children they had not seen for several years.

On November 10, 1942, word was received that the children would be able to leave Persia. As preparations began for departure, necessary travel items were distributed. The hoarding continued as napkins, tubes of toothpaste, clothing, shoes, and even rags. The black market continued to operate as tomatoes were exchanged for apples and eggs were sold for pennies. Mouldy bread continued to be kept under beds. The children could not be broken of their survival instincts that had been honed over many months of horror. The Polish authorities had promised aid, as these children were still Polish citizens. Warm clothing for the coming winter and shoes were all supposed to arrive, but few supplies ever did.

Finally, after the usual lengthy bureaucratic delays by the British authorities, the immigration certificates arrived. On January 3, 1943, 716 children, with adult escorts, all of whom were refugees in one sense or another, began their journey to Palestine. They were all loaded onto military trucks and travelled over rocky roads to an Iranian port called Bandar Shahpour on the Persian Gulf. The bedraggled children were then loaded onto a freighter which after a difficult journey arrived in Karachi, Pakistan.

One must understand the perils and limits of war to grasp the difficulty of the voyage. Both the Germans and the Japanese were still victorious on many fronts. The fierce battle at Stalingrad in Russia did not end until February 1943. So the great turning points of World War II were just being reached. Great care had to be taken to transport these seven hundred children.

The ongoing war restricted both the naval and air passage for these precious children. Still, the youngsters went wild as the ship left, jumping, screaming, singing, and yelling as they experienced the salty air and waves. Their counsellors had a hard time restraining them. Even though there were no beds, only hammocks and the blankets, the children were not just happy—they were ecstatic. They were used to far worse.

After some weeks of adequate food, the hoarding and thefts decreased. They sat at long tables in a somewhat orderly fashion. All the hidden food was given to the stevedores, who unloaded the ship in Karachi. The lice came back in full force and constant fumigation had to be practiced. Soon they were encamped in Karachi. Everyone was overwhelmed with the huge crowds that besieged their camp. Most of them were beggars and they had to be driven away with force. Even more draining was the heat. The two weeks in Karachi were more than enough for the children. They soon departed from Karachi for the Red Sea and the Suez Canal. When they arrived at Suez in the Canal Zone they were disembarked, to be loaded onto trains that would take them across the Sinai Desert to the Egyptian-Palestinian border.

On February 18, 1943, the Tehran children arrived at the Atlit refugee camp in northern Palestine. The train that brought them across the Sinai desert was surrounded by thousands of well-wishers. The entire Yishuv turned out to greet the tired and weary children. Thousands cheered, danced, and sang to welcome the new additions.

The entire Jewish community was moved by the experience. Word had reached the Yishuv of the horrors that faced the Jewish people in Poland and other places. While comprehension of the Shoah was still not yet complete, many were aware in 1943 of what the rumours of gassings, mass shootings, and death camps really meant. For a few days, joy prevailed throughout the land.

The homecoming was a momentous event in the short history of the Yishuv. Joyous reunions with long-lost relatives marked the occasion. On the journey to Atlit, crowds of thousands surged around the train, showering the children with oranges and candies. Hundreds of Jewish volunteers welcomed the children with glowing faces. A huge banner saying "Welcome Home" greeted the exhausted children.

Many of the children were subsequently adopted and some found their families. Many served with distinction in Israel's armed forces and more than forty-five died for their new homeland. It was a momentous diversion from the increasing horrible news about the Shoah.

A second transport of 110 additional children arrived overland via Iraq on August 28, 1943. In total, some 870 "Tehran children" arrived and were saved from the Holocaust by coming to British Mandate Palestine. The children were dispersed to *kibbutzim* (collective farms) and *moshavim* (cooperative farming villages) throughout the land. A few managed to find their parents and others found relatives, but for the most part they remained orphans. Thirty-five of the Tehran children died as either soldiers or civilians in the Israeli War of Independence from 1948 to 1949.

The Tehran children with sun helmets.

A Tehran child with meager belongings.

The Tehran Children, finally being fed properly.

The Tehran children singing Hatikvah.

The Tehran children on a train in the Sinai.

The Tehran children with Jewish guides.

The Tehran children close to liberation.

CHAPTER 8

The *Struma*

Some sixty-five years after the close of World War II and the concurrent slaughter of 6 million Jewish people, including 1.5 million children, a wide net of blame has been cast. Clearly the Nazis and their collaborators murdered the Jews, but who stood by and what could they have done? Who acquiesced to these horrible crimes?

Much blame has been heaped on Franklin Delano Roosevelt and the wartime American government. Clearly the Roosevelt Administration could have done much more. It might have been possible, especially in 1944, to bomb Auschwitz or other places of death. The rail lines might have been destroyed. Numerous rescue proposals could have been accepted or merely even explored. Ransom demands and countless other solutions were offered.

In the end, there was really only one safe haven for the Jews of Europe: Palestine. This one attainable refuge to which European Jewry could escape was controlled by the British Government. The policies of His Majesty's Government from 1933 to1948 sealed the fate of perhaps a million Jews. One of the saddest stories of that era was that of the *Struma*. On the morning of February 24, 1942, an explosion ripped through a decrepit ship barely afloat, jam packed with almost eight hundred Jewish refugees. This is the sad story of the passengers, the ship, and the Jewish people. It was also a time that Britain, Turkey, and others would like to forget.

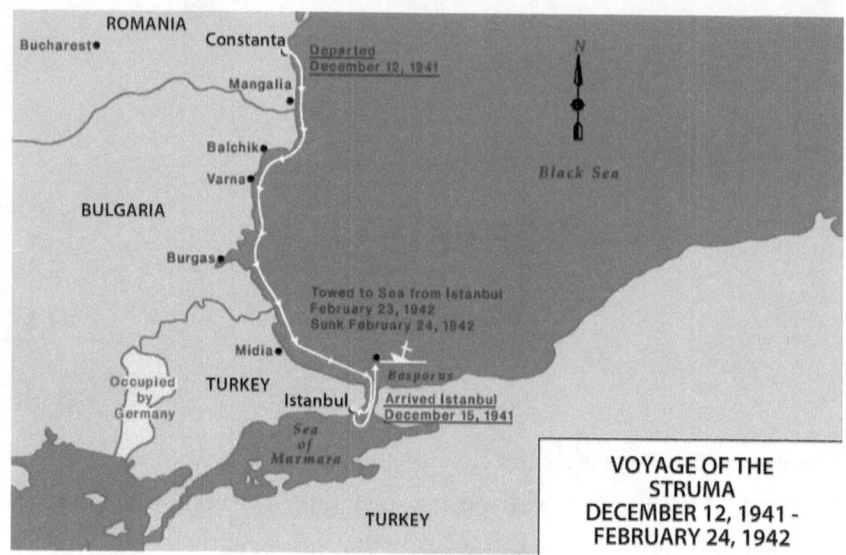

Voyage of the ship Struma

From 1934 to 1938, 165,000 Jews had emigrated to British Mandate Palestine, mainly from Western and Central Europe, with many coming from Germany. The Arab Revolt in Palestine from 1935 to 1938 prompted a harsh response from the British towards both the Arabs and the Jews. For the Arabs the British responded with assassinations, machine gunning from airplanes, the destroying of crops and orchards, the demolition of numerous homes, and endless security checkpoints. At the same time, the British restrictions on Jewish immigration grew even tighter. As usual, the British were concerned about Arab reaction, their oil supply, and strategic considerations like the Suez Canal. A series of White Papers issued by the British further restricted Jewish immigration to the Holy Land.

Among the new restrictions was the possession of an immigration certificate, which had to be purchased at a price of about 1000 pounds each, an unbelievable sum in the 1930s and 1940s. It was at this time that the British blockade was established around Palestine. Dozens of ships were turned back and many thousands of people lost their lives as a result of the inability to penetrate the blockade. No immigration ships were allowed.

For many, this was the start of bitter Jewish terrorism against the British and the founding of the Irgun, the Stern Gang, and other groups. All these organizations were condemned for terrorism against the British without remembering the context of the destruction of European Jewry and their inability to escape the vast prison camp that Europe had become.

In December 1941, Reinhard Heydrich was planning his infamous conference at Wansee, where the so-called Final Solution was organized. The meeting was then postponed until January 1942 because of Pearl Harbour. After the conference, the Jews of Europe were doomed, as the proposals of the Final Solution were implemented.

The British-Jewish conflict reached a climax in British Mandate Palestine. Several large illegal immigration ships were prepared, as people were clamouring to get out of Europe at any cost. Thousands of Jewish refugees were preparing to leave the port of Constanza on Romania's Black Sea Coast, now sometimes a cruise port.

One such ship was the *Struma*, whose story begins in Romania during the Shoah. Romania was an ally of Nazi Germany during World War II and was the place where some of the most horrific atrocities of the Shoah were committed. For a long time Romania had been a bitterly anti-Semitic country. In 1927, the Legion of Archangel Michael had been founded. One of its principal aims was to prosecute, harass, and murder Jews. The atrocities committed by the Romanians were so bad that the SS stepped in and stopped them. They did not like the public displays people being burned alive and hanged from meat hooks in public places as part of wild pogroms. The Nazis preferred their quiet, efficient, industrialized genocide, where 10,000 people per day could be efficiently processed, stripped of their valuables, gassed, and then incinerated.

In August 1940 a new law was instituted in Romania by King Carol II. It defined a Jew in the broadest possible way, broader even than the Nazi definition. Major restrictions were also placed on the Jews of Romania. Later in 1940, the new Prime Minister of Romania forced the king out and invited the German troops into the country. Romania then became even more pro-Nazi. The Germans were anxious to protect their sources of oil in Romania. It seemed that the Jewish people had once again landed on the wrong side of oil interests.

In the mean time, the fascist Iron Guard went on a rampage and pogroms were committed all over Romania. In February 1941, Romania entered the war on the German side. A last refugee ship from Romania, the *Darian II*, picked up survivors from a ship, the *Salvador*, and made its way to Haifa, packed with eight hundred terrified Jews. The *Darian II* was intercepted by a British patrol boat and escorted to Haifa. The ship was towed to Cyprus, where everyone was detained.

In this terrible historical context, a number of wealthy and middle-class Romanian Jews, all desperate to flee, began to negotiate with a Greek ship owner, Aristotle Pandelis. They wanted to escape from Romania at any cost. Pandelis, the Greek shipping agent responsible for the *Struma*, said, "I am not running a cruise line and I can't change regular prices. You must pay and pay big to get Jews out. Then you will save them!" Pandelis placed newspaper ads for the *Struma* in order to entice passengers. The low original price for a ticket was $100 USD (still a vast sum then), but lies and delays in the sailing date caused the price to rise. A false inspection report was prepared. Pandelis promised passengers an onboard hospital, nurses, doctors, good wholesome food, ten toilets (there were only two for eight hundred people), and a safe ship. In reality, the ship was clearly unseaworthy, the engine did not work, and the hull leaked. The *Struma* had never carried passengers or human cargo of any kind. It was really a cattle boat. Nevertheless, the passenger list filled up as eight hundred terrified Jews bought their tickets, desperate to flee Romania and get to Palestine, the Promised Land. A specially sealed train carrying the Jews left Bucharest, the capital of Romania, and made its way to Constanza, where they were to board the *Struma*. Upon arrival at Constanza, a Mrs. Claudia Bloch and her family came to the embarkation pier. The elderly grandmother of the family looked at the ship, grimaced, and simply refused to go on board.

In the meantime, the British Government agonized in some ways about its policies and immigration to Palestine. Churchill intervened with the British Navy not to deport Jews to faraway places like Mauritius and to treat them decently, as the refugees that they were. He was disturbed to hear that they were being held in concentration camps. Churchill had said on no account were they to be sent back from where they had originated.

Some refugees had already been sent to Mauritius, which was riddled with malaria, while others were sent to Cyprus. Churchill said in a quote about the Arabs, "I wonder if their attachment to our cause is so slender that a few acts of charity to the Jews will dislodge their loyalty." Winston Churchill was right.

But the British military staff was adamant in not allowing Jewish refugees into Palestine. The British High Command simply said the Jews could not challenge the government. Sir Harold MacMichael, the British High Commissioner for Palestine, had a death sentence put on his head by the Irgun, and another superior British officer was eventually assassinated. When the refugees were forcibly moved from place to place there were incredible scenes of brutality and ill treatment. Many subsequently died of disease. There were many allegations by the British that the refugees were infiltrated by Nazi agents. Even the *Saturday Evening Post*, a respected American commercial magazine, ran a lengthy exposé on German Nazis, who supposedly had a special school in Prague where SS officers were taught Yiddish, circumcised, taught to pray, and made to wear skull caps. Hundreds of these Nazi agents were to be sprinkled amongst the Jewish refugees; however, not one such agent was ever found.

On August 24, 1941, Winston Churchill broadcasted on the BBC the early reports of the Shoah. The German radio codes had been cracked, and the British knew what was going on behind the lines in Russia. The mass shootings by the *Einsatzgruppen* that marked the beginning of Shoah were known to the Allied governments. On November 25, 1942, the first reports of what eventually became the Holocaust appeared in the *Palestine Post*. The front page stated that there had been "mass butchery of Polish Jews." Noteworthy was that this description stated that it was unsubstantiated. Clearly disbelief and a lack of comprehension still permeated the Palestinian Jewish community. A much clearer dispatch appeared in July 1944, which stated that 400,000 Hungarian Jews were being sent to death camps in Poland.

In the summer of 1941, one eventual passenger of the *Struma*, David Stoliar, was a strong eighteen-year-old conscripted into digging trenches for the Romanian army. He was always a great swimmer and extremely strong, characteristics that would serve him well on the coming journey. The eight-hundred passengers on the sealed train from Bucharest finally arrived in Constanza. It took three days for the passengers to board the ship. Generally the "passengers" were supposed to be allowed to take 20 kg (44 lbs), this was reduced by half. The Romanian guards looted the passengers. Stoliar had bought a thick leather jacket, which he wore at all times to avoid it being weighed. Watches and jewellery were taken from the refugees. They were told they would not need their things where they were going. Then the passengers saw the *Struma* as it really was, an old cattle carrier with a rotten wooden hull. The so called bunks were what you would associate with Auschwitz. Finally the decrepit engine turned over after a tug boat had pulled the ship out to sea. Passengers jammed their way onto the deck. They began to sing Hatikvah, the song of hope and the future Israeli national anthem. All were glad to be free of Nazi-occupied Europe and looking forward to their new homeland in Eretz, British Mandate Palestine, soon to become Israel. Despite the conditions, optimism prevailed and spirits were buoyant. oon after their departure the engine failed and the ship was left drifting. The initial tugboat came along and the engine was inspected. The tugboat crew wanted about 10,000 American dollars to fix the engine. Rings, watches, necklaces, and all kinds of jewellery again were collected. They paid the mechanics and finally the engine turned over and the ship was on its way. The ship had left on December 12, 1941. On December 15, 1941, the ship somehow bumped its way to Istanbul. Passengers were not allowed ashore and the ship was quarantined for two long months.

Turkey was neutral during World War II but had a pro-Nazi bias. It was a secular Moslem country. As a neutral country, Turkey was in a dilemma. The Germans had mined the harbours and the straits of the Dardanelles in an effort to prevent the Russians from getting any aid through the Dardanelles and the Black Sea. The Russians, on the other hand, didn't want the Germans getting Chromium, an important steel hardener available only in Turkey. So the Russians patrolled the Black Sea with submarines to cut supplies of this valuable trace metal. The *Struma* and its passengers were caught in between the British blockade of Palestine, the Germans, the blood-thirsty Romanians, the neutral, uncaring Turks, and the Russians, each having their own war aims.

As always, the Jews were the expendable pawns. The *Struma* presented a particular dilemma for the British, who were determined not to allow Jewish immigration to Palestine. At one point, serious British proposals were advanced to sink the *Struma*. Winston Churchill and cooler heads prevailed. The *Struma* sat unwanted by anyone. The Turks decided that the ship was legally able to sail through the straits from the Black Sea to the Mediterranean and eventually to Haifa. But the British were adamant—no Jewish refugees allowed in Palestine. In the meantime, on the *Struma*, food was running low, people were sick, conditions were deteriorating, and the spirits of the passengers were flagging. Would they be sent back to Romania? Interned on Cyprus? Or even worse?

Some Turkish citizens did care, there always being a Tikun Olam[12] who wants to save people and do the right thing. One Turkish consular officer who was not Jewish, Needef Kent, intervened in Paris when a boxcar full of Turkish Jewish refugees was being organized to go to Auschwitz. Kent went on the boxcar and simply refused to get off. SS Nazi officials, anxious not to antagonize the Turks and wanting to keep them neutral, finally relented and let the Jews go.

In the meantime, Istanbul's Jewish community rallied to the cause of the marooned *Struma*. Food and other supplies were collected and taken to the stricken ship. The ship's passengers had a diet of bread and salted, dried herring. Finally some oranges were smuggled aboard. The oranges were a prized possession. The passengers had a New Year's party during which the Captain, a Bulgarian, got drunk. Moved by his passengers' singing and dancing, he got up swaying drunkenly and pledged he would never abandon his passengers and his ship, loudly proclaiming, "I will take you to Haifa!"

---

[12] Tikun Olam: a person who wants to save the world

The ship remained in quarantine in the harbour of Istanbul as police boats circled it and passengers cried out for help. Little was known about the *Struma* in the outside world. A few passengers, fewer than ten, had outside connections. They got off the ship and an appeal was made to sympathetic British consular officials to issue visas at least for the children, but time dragged on. On February 16, 1942, His Majesty's Government approved visas for all children between the ages of eleven and sixteen to go to Palestine, provided that they were not Nazi spies. The Turkish government intervened, as the British had no ship to transport the refugees, the *Struma* was not seaworthy, and no one seem to care what would happen to the passengers. Negotiations dragged on. The Turkish government said that the British must provide a ship to take the children. Many of the passengers were on the verge of committing suicide. The engine still did not work.

Churchill tried to intervene on the Jews' behalf, but even the appeals of a British prime minister were lost in the British bureaucracy. The Turkish government issued a deadline of February 16, by which time the ship had to leave Istanbul, regardless of whether the children got off or not. On that same sad day, the British government had issued visas for the children provided that they weren't Nazi spies. The Turkish government then said that the children would not be allowed to go overland through Turkey and Syria to Palestine. The *Struma* had now been at anchor in Istanbul for two months.

When the deadline arrived, a Turkish military tugboat and a police boat came alongside the *Struma*. Two police men boarded the ship to secure a line. The passengers resisted and threw the two policemen overboard. More police boats arrived, and a hundred heavily armed policemen boarded the ship and secured a line to the tugboat. The *Struma* was towed about 12 miles out to sea before the line was cut. The ship was left to drift aimlessly in the water. The Turkish government had never told the British government what they were going to do, as one British consular official forlornly waited, on the dock, for the visas for the children.

On the morning of February 24, a Russian submarine spied the *Struma*. Stalin had issued strict orders that no neutral shipping was to be allowed on the Black Sea because of the Chromium issue. The ship was torpedoed. A massive explosion occurred and the leaking hull flew apart. Most of the survivors were unable to swim and the water was icy cold. In the meantime, the British Foreign Office had sent a telegram to their embassy in Ankara to delay the sailing of the ship so they could deal with the admission of the children. It was too late; the children were at the bottom of the Black Sea. The two lifeboats on the ship were destroyed in the explosion. There were a few survivors, clinging to pieces of wood in icy cold waters until their fingers froze and they sank. David Stoliar was wearing his heavy leather jacket, the same jacket that he had never wanted to get weighed. It saved his life. The first mate and David Stoliar managed to clamber aboard a floating wooden bench. After twenty-four hours, the first mate, Lazar Bikor, became unconscious and slipped into the sea. As the bench drifted, David saw a lighthouse more than a mile away and began to swim towards it. While swimming for shore, a small ship passed him and waved flags at the shore to signal for a rowboat to be sent. David Stoliar was the sole survivor of the *Struma* as more than eight hundred people, Jewish refugees from Nazi Europe, drowned.

For three days David recuperated. Slowly he was nursed back to health by a small village of Moslem fisherman. Finally David was put on a commercial bus going to Istanbul. The bus was filled with chattering chickens and loud talkative peasants carrying their produce. When David got to Istanbul, he was immediately arrested by the Turkish authorities as he had no visa and no papers.

The sinking of the *Struma* brought forth a landslide of abuse against the British. No one knew that it was a Russian submarine that sank the ship. The British and the Turks blamed the Romanian government, as after all the passengers were Romanian. The British press strongly blamed their government. A series of posters were put up in Jerusalem saying, "Wanted for the murder of 500 innocent people, Sir Harold MacMichael, the British High Commissioner."[13] The Irgun and the Lehi, both radical Jewish groups, did try to kill him twice. Unlike Lord Moyne, who said, "What would I do with a million Jews?"[14], Harold MacMichael survived the war. Lord Moyne was assassinated in Cairo in 1944 by Lehi agents.

The *Struma*, like the *Exodus 1947*, was a turning point in British-Jewish relations in Mandate Palestine. People like Menachem Begin and Yitzhak Shamir were emboldened, and a reign of terror started against the British.

David Stoliar stayed in jail for six weeks and then was released and made his way through Syria to Palestine. He took odd jobs in British Mandate Palestine. In 1943, David Stoliar went to Cairo and joined the British army to fight the Nazis. After surviving the British Armed Forces for three years, in 1946 he lived for a time in Israel and then went on to become a successful entrepreneur.

The Struma—Istanbul Harbour 1942 (From Turkish newspaper)

---

[13] It is interesting to note that the death toll on the posters was incorrect, placing the number of dead at 500 instead of 800.

[14] A quote made by Lord Moyne after attempts were made to ransom Hungarian Jews by Adolf Eichmann.

The Struma—Overcrowded with refugees.

CHAPTER 9

The Sailboats

The desperation of the Jews of Europe was such that they considered every possible means of escape. In many cases, large ships were not available. As a result, many Jews turned to sailboats. These tiny, barely seaworthy ships were to become lifeboats to flee Nazi-occupied Europe.

Alexandra Gomulka described her voyage on the *Mircea*. Alexandra was born in Bucharest, Romania, in 1939. She came from an upper-middle-class Romanian Jewish family. Romania was an ally of Nazi Germany and had participated in horrible atrocities against its Jewish inhabitants. The Jews, besides being tortured and killed, were put into forced labour battalions. Even the snow shovelling in Bucharest was done by Jews, held at gunpoint. Constant beatings marked the lives of the Romanian Jews. It was clear to the Jews that they had to get out by any means possible.

In the winter of 1942, forty desperate people pooled their resources and bought a sailboat, the *Mircea*. Their ages ranged from two to seventy years old, and all bore exit visas from Paraguay (a landlocked country in South America). The all-Jewish crew consisted of four Jewish *schlemazels* (fools) and an incapable captain. Although the captain dressed the part, with the usual navy white uniform and trappings, he had no relevant experience and was incompetent. Two Jewish engineers who would not go on the voyage refitted the *Mircea*. Every passenger was very fearful and their friends and relatives predicted a disaster. The forty Romanian Jews were mainly businesspeople involved in textiles. The *Mircea*, hardly a dreadnought type ship, had a top speed of 5 MPH and was about 40 feet long.

Provisions were assembled and the luggage was put on board by the crew of fools. As expected the last remaining and most precious possessions of the passengers were in their meagre pieces of luggage. Several pieces of the prized luggage fell in the water, irretrievably lost. Still the crew complained that the luggage took up too much space. As the boat departed, the beleaguered passengers heard the departing messages from the bystanders on the shore, "The crazies won't even make it to Istanbul."

They had left on Friday, April 10, 1942, from a tiny Romanian port called Tulcea. The next day the voyagers arrived in Solana, Romania, where they were guided through a minefield. Soon they made their way out to the Black Sea, where numerous seagulls seemed to be accompanying them. Seagulls are considered to be a sign of nautical good luck. On Sunday, April 12, they passed Constanza, presently a cruise port in Romania. Sunday was marked by the marriage of the Mendrovitches. The supposed captain performed the ceremony, with one wise passenger observing, "He is really not a captain, but then again this is not a ship or even a proper boat."

At about six o'clock in the evening, as darkness began to fall, a Romanian naval vessel, the *Avizu*, opened fire on the *Mircea*. The Romanians, allies of the Germans, thought the *Mircea*'s passengers were Russians. After torturous negotiations, the crew of the *Avizu* was convinced that the passengers were legitimate refugees heading through the Black Sea for the Dardanelles. The Paraguayan visas were given as proof of their final destination. How anyone could have believed that people going to Paraguay would be travelling there via the Black Sea is hard to fathom.

On Monday, April 13, the *Mircea* was in the open sea with no land in sight. On Tuesday they spotted the Turkish shore, but engine problems developed as both the pump and carburetor began faltering. A mechanic on board named Komarowsky managed to keep the boat functioning, although he was sea sick most of the time.

On their passage they saw a mine laid by one of many Russian submarines that patrolled the Black Sea to prevent the transfer of chromium from Turkey to Germany. The ship stopped for the night to avoid crossing the Bosporus in the dark. The passengers listened to the shortwave radio, and they were all moved to hear Radio Free France's sign off—the "Marseillaise" (the French national anthem).

On the morning of Wednesday, April 15, 1942, the *Mircea* passed through the Bosporus and heard gun shots from the Turkish shore. They dropped anchor in the Sea of Marmora and spent the night on the water listening to classical music from Radio Bucharest.

Friday, April 17, was described as Black Friday. The seas became very stormy. They tried to dock during the storm and were driven off by armed Turkish police officers shooting at them. They were unable to take on much needed food and water.

On Saturday, April 18, they entered the Aegean Sea, and for the first time it became very hot. They arrived in the Turkish port of Smyrna. They were able to take on some provisions and Mr. Dafkovitz, the representative of the Jewish Agency, came to see them. On Monday, April 20, they heard on the radio that it was Hitler's birthday.

They continued to have difficulty replenishing their supplies as the Turkish authorities refused to give them more than a few olives and some water. The Turkish police forced them to leave, and on the way out of port they hit a fancy yacht called the *Valdora* (another example of the not-so-great seamanship of the *Mircea*'s crew). The weather continued to be stormy and a notation was made that the current was stronger than the decrepit engine.

Eventually they reached Rhodes and entered a beautiful bay with snow-covered mountains in the background. They raised flags to indicate that they were refugees. By mistake, they raised the wrong flag, indicating they had explosives on board. Having survived that incident, they passed their time listening to Hitler's speeches on the shore radio and playing chess. At night this brave group of Jewish refugees had a concert. One passenger played a violin and another played an accordion. They sang and a boatload of nearby Turkish sailors joined in the singing.

The Italian navy was in control of this area, and although the Italians were friendly, the voyagers on the *Mircea* were placed under arrest. An Italian officer listened politely as the beleaguered Jews explained patiently that they were refugees who leaving Romania and had valid passports and exit visas to Paraguay. Finally the Italian officer opened the door and shouted, "*Siete libere!*" You are free! The Italians then guided them through another of the many minefields.

As they continued the journey, an Italian naval patrol vessel encountered them. Alexandra Gomulka's father was terrified that the Italians would think that they were a small warship. Alexandra's father held the three-year-old child aloft and waved a white flag to show the patrol vessel they were refugees and friendly. The Italians came along side and gave them food and water.

Despite the Fascist nature of wartime Italy, and in spite of any proclamations made by Mussolini, the Italian dictator, the Italians had no real interest in killing Jews. In fact, Italian Jews had the highest survival rates of any group of Jews in Nazi-occupied Europe. In addition, Italian soldiers in a series of remarkable displays saved foreign-born Jews from the Nazis in occupied southern France and Greece.

Disputes arose amongst the *Mircea's* passengers. As they passed Cyprus one man wanted to get off and still another insisted that they must go directly to Palestine. However they knew if they reached Cyprus the passengers would be immediately detained. They all decide to continue on to Palestine.

They ran out of fuel and were very low on food. Another boat offered fuel for $2600 US. The *Mircea's* passengers refused the fuel and instead bought a little bread. Eventually they bought some fuel from the passing boat and continued on their journey. As the *Mircea* closed in on the shore of British Mandate Palestine shore near Haifa, a British patrol boat with sirens stopped them. Their long and difficult journey ended with the entire group of Jewish refugees being interned in Atlit, a British detention camp in Palestine. After some months in captivity they were allowed into the Mandate, but their numbers were counted against the ever-present immigration quotas.

Michael Ruletta described in his memoirs a very similar journey in a sailboat called the *Euxin*. The *Euxin* was built as a pleasure craft for upper-class Romanians sailing along the Romanian and Bulgarian shores of the Black Sea. Besides its sails, the *Euxin* had a second-hand Ford motor to provide auxiliary propulsion.

Before his journey Ruletta described the same sort of Romanian and Nazi atrocities as the passengers of the *Mircea*. He had seen horrible massacres, including Jews hanged from hooks in slaughterhouses. It was said that the Romanian atrocities were so bad that the Nazi SS had to step in and appeal to the Romanians to not to make the murder of Jews so public.

Ruletta and his group of family and friends pondered how to escape. Overland routes through Bulgaria, Turkey, and then Syria were closed. Their group of twelve had prolonged negotiations with the two Greeks who had built the *Euxin* regarding prices and supplies. Two of the group obtained genuine visas for Ecuador, another South American country. The rest made do with fraudulent exit visas. The Romanian government was well aware of the fraudulent pedigree of the visas, but they condoned it and were happy to receive the funds for the visas. In addition, the authorities wanted to maintain a semblance of order even though bribery was the common practice. Two strong stipulations made the exit visas even more difficult to obtain. Firstly, the bearer of the visa had to leave Romania within fifteen days of the visa's issuance or be deported to a war zone. Secondly, the Turkish authorities wanted a Palestinian visa from the British. Somehow the fleeing refugees felt that if they could get on Turkish soil they would be allowed transit rights through to the Mandate.

The group received tremendous cooperation with their paperwork from Jewish Agency officials in Istanbul. Turkey was a neutral country in World War II, and the Jewish Agency was allowed to operate there.

Finally, after seven months of secret preparations, they were ready to start their perilous journey. On March 14, 1941, Ruletta and the other passengers took a train from Bucharest to Constanza, the Romanian port on the Black Sea. It was still bitter winter when they left, and they watched elderly Jews being beaten and forced to shovel snow in Bucharest. When they arrived in Constanza the boat was stacked with smoked beef, oil, flour, biscuits, coffee in tins, and sardines. Each person was allowed only three garments and they kept only their gold wedding rings, selling their gold wristwatches.

The *Euxin* departed on March 17, 1941, in frigid conditions carrying thirteen passengers and three crewmembers, all of whom were dressed in ski clothes for warmth. On March 20, 1941, the ship entered the Bosporus and began its passage towards the Mediterranean. As they came into view of the Turkish shore, a grey police patrol boat filled with officers brandishing revolvers stopped the *Euxin* from proceeding. The ship was running low on the essentials of food, fuel, and especially water. Two of the three man crew decided to go on strike. The two sailors seized a dingy and rowed away to a Greek island. The remainder of the passengers encountered a gale that further impeded their progress.

The boat ran aground at Celik, a small Romanian peasant community. The peasants were very friendly and welcomed the fugitives. Eventually they found their way to Cesme, Turkey, a Red Cross camp for refugees. The refugees remained stranded for a long time at Cesme. Appeals were continually made to a Jewish Labour MP in England named Joshua Wedgewood, to whom they had a connection. Nevertheless the passengers of the *Euxin* were trapped at Cesme, where conditions were very difficult for the fifteen thousand refugees kept there.

Ruletta and his fellow passengers cooked using the Greek liqueur ouzo for their primus stove. They subsisted on lettuce, tomatoes, sheep and goat meat, as well as some halva. The weather became so hot that they began to swim.

The group in the camp was stricken with fear as they heard of German advances in North Africa. Concern was strongly expressed that Rommel and his Panzers might even reach Palestine. Finally they received a cable from the British consul in Itzmin. All of them were given British visas to get to Cyprus, but not to Palestine.

The *Euxin* was underway again with a new captain, a Turkish man named Miephesta. They disobeyed British instructions and set sail for Palestine while grilling fish on an open fire. All the passengers said the fish was delicious as they made their way towards their ultimate goal of Palestine. A British patrol boat stopped them off the shore of Lebanon.[15] The group confessed the truth—that they wanted to go to Palestine and not Cyprus. Nevertheless they were shipped to Larnaca, Cyprus.

By the time they had reached Cyprus all the passengers were infected with lice, requiring the boat to be fumigated, and the passengers forced to

---

[15]   At this point ruled by the Vichy French

take numerous showers with carbolic soup. The hardy group of refugees were all disembarked in Cyprus and taken into custody by the British authorities. They were interned in a deluxe hotel in Larnaca in September 1942 and eventually made their way to Palestine in March 1944.

Claudia Bloch was born in Czernowicz, Bukovina, Romania, in February 1938. As a result of her grandmother's foresight and vision, Bloch did not leave Romania on the ill-fated *Struma*, but like most Jews in Romania she still wanted to desperately flee.

Claudia's earliest childhood memories were those of her parents' home in Czernowicz. She remembered most of all her mother and father's green stone fireplace, which adorned their bedroom. Her family were traditional observant Jews, and her father was described as a *tzaddik* (a righteous man). He had been educated in Vienna as an agricultural specialist and was an expert in sugar beet cultivation.

In September 1942, after refusing passage on the *Struma*, a group of 120 middle-class Jews, in a story similar to the other sailboat stories mentioned above, purchased a large sailboat with an auxiliary motor, the *Vitriol*. It sailed from Constanza in September 1942 at the height of the German victories in both Europe and Africa. Soon the over capacity boat began to list and take on water. It soon sank, but it did so in sight of the Turkish shore, meaning almost everyone on board was saved.

The passengers scrambled ashore to be aided by the Turkish military. Everyone was wet and freezing. Coats and blankets were put over the shivering passengers, young and old alike. The Turkish military personnel provided large candles, which helped warm them as they fought to get closer to the blazing bonfires that were also lit. Soon carts and donkeys were brought to transport the shipwrecked passengers to nearby villages. To compound the problems faced by these refugees, it began to pelt rain. Even the precious bread that they carried was soaked, and many people went on to contract typhoid and a few died. They were accommodated in a large hall, and eventually hot food was brought. Claudia still has a memory sixty-nine years later of her father bringing her hot soup.

The Turkish authorities decided to allow the illegal immigrants to go overland to Palestine, but via Cyprus. This group was amongst the first group of Jewish refugees to arrive in Cyprus. The simple memory of a child was that Cyprus was good. Claudia Bloch and her large extended family—consisting of three grandparents, two aunts, two uncles and still another child—lived in high style in a villa on the island. Bloch and her family had arrived before the British had built the concentration-like camps that later dotted Cyprus. The Bloch family experienced no barbed wire, watchtowers, stockades, armed guards, or vicious dogs, which characterized the later British internment of illegal Jewish refugees. The villa for the Bloch family was a large one and was extremely comfortable, and the Blochs remained in Cyprus from September 1942 to March 1944.

A highlight of the Blochs' time in Cyprus was the visit by the Jewish Brigade.[16] For a six-year-old to see a Jewish soldier must have been a transformative experience. The food in their long sojourn in Cyprus was essentially good and nourishing. Every Friday the family had to report to the police station as illegal immigrants. They hiked the island and found it a beautiful place. Bloch's father, despite all their limitations, made it an idyllic life for the family in Cyprus.

Eventually, in 1944, they were taken in a large vessel to Palestine. Soon they were disembarked at Atlit, the British detention centre for illegal immigrants. Atlit was not Cyprus and had barbed wire, stockades, watchtowers, armed guards, and guard dogs. The British controlled the perimeter of Atlit while the Zionists were in charge inside. After six weeks in Atlit they were enumerated in the immigration quota and allowed to go into Palestine. Their first days in Palestine were very exciting and they seemed to integrate well. Another childhood memory of British Mandate Palestine was their laundry room being on the top floor so that laundry could immediately be dried in the sun. The stories of these three sailboats, the *Mircea,* the *Euxin*, and the *Vitrol*, all ended in Palestine. The three groups of people who travelled on them were able to see the independence of the new Israeli state.

---

[16]   Late in the war, Winston Churchill approved a special brigade of Jewish soldiers with Stars of David on their shoulder patches. The Jewish brigade served in Italy.

The tales of the three sailboats in many ways exemplify the desperate straits of the Jewish people in Nazi occupied Europe. Here were three disparate but similar groups. They were all middle-class or upper-middle-class people. They had money, connections, and the wherewithal and courage to make decisions and carry them through. They were unlike the masses of Polish Jews, who, while they had courage, did not have the money, the connections, or the knowledge to make bold plans like those of the passengers of the sailboats.

Here were people ready to risk their lives on three unseaworthy boats. None of the boats ever had ample provisions of food or even fuel for their decrepit motors. They could take hardly anything with them, and yet they ventured forth on perilous journeys simply to escape the Nazis. Many of them were not committed Zionists, yet they were ready to make a long and very difficult voyage through very hostile waters to safety in a land, Palestine, that would be very foreign to them.

All of them experienced the same dangers. They were fired upon by the Turkish military and police, who were anxious to prevent their country from being a refuge for those fleeing the Nazis. They were mistaken for warships by Romanians, who fired upon them. The Italians who patrolled the seas, while somewhat friendly to Jewshad a tendency to mistake the sailboats for warships. The boats were also in constant danger of being found by the Germans. Finally, the Russians had mined the Black Sea extensively and patrolled it with submarines.

Despite the dangers from five different possible enemies, these intrepid sailors set out on their voyages. The young and the very old all participated. These brave Jews knew their only possible salvation and their only possible sanctuary could be British Mandate Palestine. Their final obstacle would be the British and their insidious blockade. Yet they were all willing to risk everything to challenge the British blockade after running the gauntlet of dangers.

An idyllic sailboat unlike that which the refugees sailed on.

CHAPTER 10

Imprisonment—Atlit and Cyprus

In addition to exiling immigrants to Mauritius or Eritrea, the British imprisoned many thousands in both Atlit in Palestine and various internment camps on Cyprus.

The Atlit camp was established by the British just before World War II as an internment camp for illegal Jewish immigrants. As Nazism had risen and the intentions of Hitler and his cohorts became clear, the impetus for illegal immigration, or Aliya Bet, became stronger. From April 1937 to September 1, 1939, when the war began, some forty-five ships brought more than 22,000 illegal immigrants from European ports to Palestine. While two ships sank and two others were captured by the British blockade, most of the remainder landed and their passengers were brought ashore in small boats by the Haganah and Revisionists. Many of the refugees who came ashore were captured by the British and interned at Atlit. Many were kept there for months, and their numbers were deducted from the Peel Commission fixed quota of 75,000 if they were admitted into Palestine. The quota had been fixed by the British administration and was not to be altered under any circumstances.

The three Shene orphans described their imprisonment in Atlit, Palestine, in the spring of 1946. It was Pesach but they remember matzah being provided. They arrived by truck to Atlit, which was surrounded by barbed wire, guard dogs, and watchtowers with searchlights. British paratroopers with red berets and short pants, many carrying Bren guns, cordoned them off and forced them through barbed wire enclosures into the camp. They were thoroughly searched, and even though they had legal immigration certificates they were forced into the Atlit camp. The camp had all the attributes of a prison. For some of the older people who had been Holocaust survivors, it was a horrific ordeal. After two weeks of meticulous checking the Shene children went on to an orphanage in Petah Tikvah.

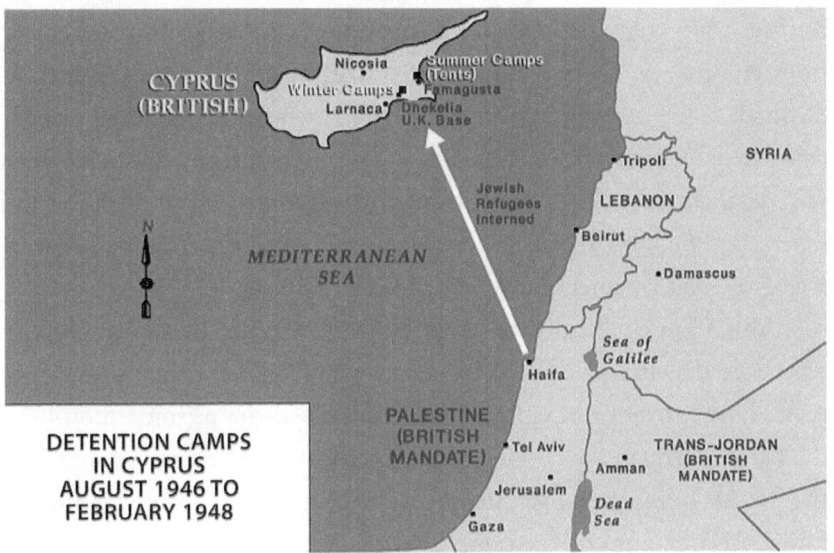

Camp locations on Cyprus

Another Holocaust survivor named Laslo Leung, who had been liberated by the Russian army, was taken to Atlit after a journey on the illegal immigration ship the *Haganah in 1947*. Leung, who had been in the Nazi camps, described Atlit with horror—the barbed wire, the watchtowers, and the decrepit barracks. While the British maintained the security perimeter of the camp, the Zionists ran the camp itself. The Jewish Agency was in charge of feeding them, and for the first time in his young life the twenty year old Leung ate tropical fruits, such as bananas, watermelons, and pomegranates. He didn't know how to eat olives, as he was not familiar with them and could not understand how to handle the pits.

Another ship came laden with refugees from Belgium and was taken to Cyprus. Many of the illegal immigrants were taken and shipped from Cyprus to Atlit. Leung was happy to see so many young girls in the next shipment. Although conditions were difficult and the British had them under heavy guard, Leung concluded it was far better than the German concentration camps. After a stay of more than two months, Leung was released into Palestine and was allowed to settle in Hadera.

Still another Holocaust survivor named Amri Sussman survived the Kastner train transport and, by a torturous rail journey, made his way from Hungary to Switzerland and eventually to northern Italy. Somehow Sussman made his way from there to Haifa, where he supposedly legally embarked. Despite his proper papers and immigration certificate, Sussman was detained in Atlit. The British went through a lengthy process of separating the legal and illegal immigrants. Eventually Amri was sent by truck to Givat Brenner where he joined the Palmach.

Both Claudia Bloch and Alex Eisen, two other illegal immigrants who were detained in Cyprus for lengthy periods spent time interned in Atlit. Their memories meshed as they described the prison atmosphere, the barely adequate food, and the harsh conditions. Everyone remembers the British being in charge outside of the camp and the Zionists and the Jewish Agency running the camp interior.

From the many testimonies, memoirs, and interviews, it can easily be concluded that Atlit was two things: a place of confinement and a place to delay immigration. Jews who did not have proper immigration certificates were going to be there until they fit into the quota. Others were put through the Atlit camp as an inspection to check them for firearms and explosives and to make sure they were not the dreaded Nazi agents. Many times an inordinate amount of time was spent checking these hapless people. Having gone through so much, one would have thought that the British would have expedited matters, especially as the war wound down.

Atlit was also used as a quarantine camp. Besides interning the illegal immigrants, even those with proper immigration certificates in the immediate postwar years were kept there for lengthy periods, ostensibly to prevent the spread of communicable diseases, such as typhoid.

Alexander Eisen was discharged after two weeks of internment in Atlit. He was given a formal document from the British authorities stating that he was a legal immigrant to Palestine. The Jewish Agency provided enough money for bus fare, and he went from Atlit to Jerusalem. He carried a small canvas bag with all his worldly possessions, including two pairs of shorts, two shirts, a pair of tefillin, and a siddur. He also had his precious electronic books in the canvas bag. Alexander Eisen started a new life in Palestine.

On October 10, 1945, a special Palmach unit of the Haganah, led by future Israeli Prime Minister Yitzhak Rabin, attacked the British internment camp at Atlit. More than two hundred prisoners were released from the jail and fled into the surrounding countryside. As a result of this daring raid, which became part of the book and film *Exodus*, the British began to intern all future illegal immigrants on Cyprus. In this way, the detainees would not be able to escape so easily. Following Rabin's daring raid, Atlit began to be used more as a quarantine camp and transit stop for the British control of the refugees.

Cyprus, a Mediterranean island about 65 km from Turkey and close to Israel, is a disputed territory between Turkey and Greece. It became the main postwar internment stop for illegal immigrants attempting to reach Palestine. At its peak there were some nine camps on Cyprus, located at two basic sites, Caroolos, north of Famagusta; and Dekhelia, just outside of Larnaca. The vast majority of the some 50,000 detainees were boat people stopped by the British blockade. Holocaust survivors supplied the majority of the refugees, with about 60 percent coming from the displaced persons camps and the rest fleeing Eastern Europe via the Bricha. It is astonishing to consider that the inmates were so young. About 80 percent of the jailed people were between the ages of thirteen and thirty-five and included six thousand orphaned children. When one considers the Holocaust as the major influence and those who survived it, the young age demographic becomes easily understandable. Again the resilience of the survivors is noteworthy, as more than two thousand children were born on Cyprus between 1946 and 1948.

Even more astonishing is the stubbornness of the British. In addition to the difficult conditions imposed by the authorities, more than eleven thousand were kept in the camps for many months after Israel's independence in May 1948. The final groups were released in January and

February 1949, eight long months after the Jewish state came into being. Britain recognized Israel in January 1949.

Frida Weller was a Polish Jew born in Nowy-Korcyn who had survived the Lodz ghetto. In the winter of 1946 Frida attempted to go to Palestine. While the ship she travelled on was large, as usual it was described as horrible. The ship, as she recounted it, was not fit for human beings, but rather "only good for animals." The motor stopped and the perilous ocean voyage took over six weeks. Everyone was sea sick on the *Chaim Alorosoltof,* named after a prewar labour leader in Palestine. She further described the hardship, explaining how everything had to be thrown overboard. As they approached the Holy Land, the British intercepted them. Following a big fight they were detained and towed to Cyprus.

Weller described Cyprus not only as a hardship but as having the attributes of a jail. She had been in the Lodz ghetto, then a work camp for the German Krupp industries near Berlin, then Ravensbruck, and finally the internment camp at Cyprus. The food was a bit better at Cyprus, and the internees ate in a general kitchen. While there was enough food it was bland and unappetizing. Frida further complained that there simply was nothing to do. You could talk and you could walk within the barbed wire enclosures. Luckily for Frida the highpoint of Cyprus was that she met her husband there and lived a long and happy life with him.

Zipora Muller, born in Czechoslovakia, went to Palestine illegally in 1946. She had been in a series of internment camps beforehand, including Bergen Belsen and Theresienstadt. Making her way through Hungary and Yugoslavia, she eventually found her way on what she described as a fishing vessel. Nevertheless some two thousand people were packed in like sardines on this ship. Again the British surrounded the vessel and detained the refugees despite their fervent resistance. The distraught passengers soon found their way to the British internment camps on Cyprus. Zipora recounted the familiar refrain of the Cyprus internment with British patrols, barbed wire, and searches culminating in release to Palestine after over three months.

Martin Branak, born in Starachowice, Poland, also found his way to Cyprus. In 1946 Branak left Italy to illegally immigrate to Palestine. He was the youngest on their unnamed ship, being only fifteen years old. In a familiar refrain, the engine of this ship burnt out, and they were caught by the British navy and towed to Cyprus. Martin recalled that they were only the second illegal Jewish ship to get to Cyprus. In contrast to others, he found his life there filled with fun. They swam almost every day, soaking up the beautiful sunshine. One of their key activities was organizing demonstrations against the British Prime Minister Clement Atlee and his unpopular foreign Minister Aneurin Bevin. Most of the detainees were very bitter against the British leaders and their unpopular Jewish immigration policies. Branak hated the British and their Cyprus camp but wryly observed that there were no gas chambers on Cyprus.

Claudia Bloch had a unique experience. Her family was one of the few that entered Cyprus during the war. Following the sinking of their illegal ship, the Blochs made their way overland through Turkey before being escorted by the British to Cyprus. Since there were no detention camps, the Bloch family were sequestered in a "five star" resort hotel in the mountains of Cyprus. They were put into a villa and the entire family of nine luxuriated in their deluxe accommodations. Some other refugee families joined them, and Claudia recalled that every family had their own dining room table and that the food was very good. Their father was even able to order special kosher food.

Every Friday before Shabbat, Bloch's father reported to the local police station. Hikes through the beautiful island occupied a lot of time, and Claudia particularly remembered the mountainous forests. They, along with the other Jewish refugees, were treated very well. A special highlight of their time on Cyprus was the visit of the Jewish Brigade. The Brigade visits seemed to be an epic event for all Jewish refugees trapped or caught in their desperate places. Aside from the Friday check-in at police headquarters there were few restrictions, and the Blochs were essentially free to wander the island as they saw fit.

In the 1980s the Bloch family staged a reunion on Cyprus. They all recalled their fond memories and their wonderful treatment. Their experience was completely the opposite of that of many postwar refugees who were interned in the nine camps that the British used on Cyprus. The illegal immigrants that were detained on Cyprus from August 1946 until after Israel's independence complained bitterly about the harsh conditions, including terrible sanitation, overcrowding, and a complete lack of privacy. A shortage of clean water, something that the British should have been able to remedy easily, was another serious issue.

Shlomo Goldhaber was born in Chernowitz, Romania. His father was a watchmaker, an elite profession among Jews. Shlomo decided to go to Israel after surviving the war. Initially he felt it was easily accessible. Little did he know that his ship would be sent to Cyprus, where he would be interned for several months. His depictions of prison camp life on Cyprus coincide exactly with all of the detainees interviewed.

Alexander Eisen was also on Cyprus and remembered two camps, one for winter and one for summer. He described the British as being "somewhat kind." It was through the camp that he was able to be in contact with his father. One of the salient memories of the internees was of the bulletin boards in the postwar period. People would post names and pictures of those missing, hoping against hope to find a connection or someone that had seen or knew of their lost relatives. Again, Alex described the British exclusion from the camps with Zionist authority prevailing in the camp. Alex had some reasonably good memories of the camps, as he learned mathematics and swimming while being held by the British. In addition, his older sister was married in Cyprus. He was happy that his mother was able to cook. He stayed four long months in Cyprus and then went to Atlit for a further two weeks.

Jacob Steindler, a Hungarian Jew born in 1923, somehow got himself to Marseille where he became part of the Bricha. In a familiar story, the illegal fishing boat captain fled with their money and the six hundred passengers were towed to Haifa by the British. They were sent by a British naval vessel to a Displaced Persons camp in Cyprus. Jacob Steindler was not at all depressed, since he wanted to get out of Europe at all costs. At least he was in Cyprus, close to Palestine and he was learning Hebrew. He was being prepared for a new life. He met his future wife, a young lady from Belgium, and together they were taken to Atlit. Eventually Jacob Steindler settled down in kibbutz Ein Harod to a life in Israel.

Edgar Bragen's recollection of Cyprus was the ten-Cypriot note with which he bribed a British officer to get better treatment. Bragen also contrasted the ill-fitting clothes of the detainees, most of them thin or emaciated, with those of the British, who were well dressed and expertly groomed. Bragen recalled the shorts, khaki socks, and well-pressed shirts providing quite a contrast to the dishevelled refugees. Nevertheless, Bragen concluded that these immaculately clothed British officers accepted bribes from the Holocaust survivors.

The stories of these displaced people are many. Edgar Bragen recalled an old man clutching an old and tattered but official-looking document. No matter what entreaties were made in the camp on Cyprus, the elderly man would not let go of his official document. It was 1947 and the man desperately wanted to go to Palestine before he died. Finally he displayed the paper to an official. It was a valid British immigration certificate, dated 1945. He was two years late; the certificate had expired. The old man languished over another year in detention at Cyprus.

The British detainment policies were cruel and malicious. The fact that they were dealing with the remnants of a people who had lost six million relatives never seems to have entered the British consciousness. The internment on Cyprus in the postwar years went beyond reasonable behaviour, even for an occupying power. To keep thousands detained on Cyprus even after Israeli Independence was simply cruel and unusual punishment. The Jewish terrorism in Palestine that the British policies inspired seems from the vantage point of many years to have been justified.

Cyprus Imprisonment.

Imprisoned refugees on Cyprus, making a Star of David to
show their hope for the future.

CHAPTER 11

Legal Immigration

Not every Jewish person who came to British Mandate Palestine did so illegally. Many were able to come before the British blockade had been put into force in 1936 from Germany and Austria. Still others were able to get immigration certificates from the British authorities. Prior to 1947, Canadian citizens travelled on British passports. One staunch Zionist, Miriam Beckerman, travelled on her British passport from Toronto, Canada, to Palestine. Miriam was born in Toronto's east end. Her father was a TTC (Toronto Transit Commission) conductor, and her mother was a seamstress. Miriam made her way through the depression of the 1930s by managing a Yiddish paper route. It was the classic upbringing of the time, *oorim* but *freilich* (poor but happy). She went to the Farbund (Labour Zionist movement); her parents were Zionists, not Yiddishists.

Beckerman went to Central Commerce and took typing and stenography, two lost arts. Years later Miriam got an advanced degree in English at York University. A lifelong Zionist Miriam was a member of Habonim, a Zionist youth group. She remembered the Friday night socials at 24 Cecil Street. These were characterised by lots of singing and Israeli dancing. These Friday night affairs cemented her strong links with labour Zionism. In 1945, Miriam Beckerman went to a mass meeting at Massey Hall to commemorate the Holocaust.

Beckerman continued to work at the Canadian Jewish Congress, where she used a Yiddish typewriter. In 1945 Miriam was in New Jersey listening to David Ben-Gurion espousing immigration to Israel. In

November 1946, prior to leaving for Palestine, she received a dedication book, a trilingual book of psalms in Yiddish, Hebrew, and English.

Beckerman departed for Palestine in December 1946 with her British passport, forestalling the need for an immigration certificate. She took with her a large steamer trunk with her name and address stencilled on it. Her parents were quite supportive and had written to her aunt in Kvar Saba. She spent two long weeks crossing the Atlantic in a converted troop ship. Miriam especially remembered the hammocks and sparse facilities.

Miriam received a great deal of aid from a Tzvi Bernstein, an architect who later designed the Dizengoff Centre. A highlight of the passage was passing through the Straits of Gibraltar. The ship that she travelled on stopped in both Athens and Beirut. Miriam found the scene at Beirut a tumultuous one with a tremendous amount of noise from people begging and selling. Finally they arrived at night in Haifa. Beyond the beauty of the city, which many had described as their first glimpse of Palestine, the aroma of the beautiful city on the Mediterranean was intoxicating.

Representatives of the Jewish Agency and the people from Kfar Blum, their ultimate destination, all met them on the dock. After staying overnight in Haifa, the group attempted the narrow primitive roads that traversed the Galilee, driving to Kfar Blum. At this point Miriam could speak some Hebrew but honed her language skills in the two months she spent at Kfar Blum. She reflected that the group she was in had to be very idealistic to settle in the country in 1947 just prior to the War of Independence. The huge steamer trunk that carried all her worldly possessions finally fell apart on its third journey when she settled in Magan Baruch, where she met her future husband. Her husband's family had immigrated to Palestine from Russia in 1925, and he was a veteran of the British Eighth Army. Miriam's husband wisely predicted the future when he concluded that there would never be peace with the Arabs.

After their marriage in 1947, her husband worked for the Port Authority in Tel Aviv. During his time on the docks he helped smuggle Czechoslovakian arms and ammunition hidden under sacks of onions into Palestine to prepare for the 1948 war. While Miriam's husband carried a great deal of animosity towards the British, she confessed that she felt no such anger. They spent six months in Ramat Gan, a suburb of Tel Aviv where their first son was born. This was a difficult time in the new Israeli state, described as the Tzena (austerity).

In 1953, Miriam and her husband, perhaps tired of the difficulties, moved back to Canada. She found leaving Israel difficult and emotional. She left behind her daughter, who simply became part of the new Israel, and eventually several grandchildren. She described being in Israel as a once-in-a-lifetime experience and was very happy that she participated in the building of a country. She has returned to Israel more than twelve times and still has strong connections to her homeland.

As a young man, Ben Miller belonged to the Young Pioneer Club in Roszech (now in the Ukraine). He became infatuated with Zionism and enlisted in the Hachsharah movement. In 1933, following preparatory work in a Hachsharah kibbutz in what was then Poland, Ben Miller received approval to move to another Hachsharah kibbutz, Grochov, near Warsaw. In a harrowing journey, Ben made his way in an open truck in the dead of winter to kibbutz Grochov. After preparation time in Gorchov, Ben finally received his immigration papers and he was able to travel from Roszech to Lvov, or Lemberg. A group of immigrants gathered there and a train of Zionist pioneers proceeded to the Black Sea port of Constanza. Just after Sukkoth 1933, the Zionist migrants gathered on a Polish ship called the *Polania* and set sail for Haifa in Palestine.

After a week's journey they arrived in Palestine to be greeted with a reception consisting of figs, dried raisins, and enormous black olives. Eventually Ben found himself in Kfar Yonah. Ben worked in cement construction and further described the building up of the infrastructure of the Yishuv. Miller continued his hard work and was recognized as a *gafir*, a special person who would carry a weapon on behalf of the British Mandate. Thus Ben Miller became a Jewish policeman. Soon they received formal army hats from Australia. He went on to win a special award as "the most achieved sportsman of the police force of the Hebrew settlements." Miller married his lifelong sweetheart, Nina, in November 1940 in Modelet, Palestine. Ben went on to live in Israel after fighting with distinction in the War of Independence until the early 1950s.

Moshe Grossinger was born in Lodz, Poland, in 1943. Like many Polish Jews, he and his family were saved because they found themselves in the Russian occupied zone of Poland. The family had always had strong Zionist connections, and following the war they found Poland to be a vast Jewish graveyard. They soon found themselves caught up in the Bricha and on the road to Venice, Italy.

After independence, in May 1948, they made their way to Haifa in the new Israeli state. Conditions in the early 1950s were extremely difficult for all, and the family found themselves with four people in a one-bedroom apartment. Nevertheless, the Grossinger family became upwardly mobile in the new state, and Moshe's father served with distinction in the 1956 Sinai campaign.

The Havara (Transfer) Agreement

Early in 1933 as the Hitler regime began its rule over Germany, which eventually culminated in the murder of millions, a controversial pact was concluded. This agreement between the Third Reich and the Yishuv in Palestine transferred some 60,000 Jews and over $100 million (about $1.7 billion in 2011 dollars) to Jewish Palestine. In return the Zionist authorities agreed to halt the worldwide Jewish-led boycott against Nazi Germany. It is not generally remembered, but the Jews, especially in America, were able in the early 1930s to put enormous economic pressure on Hitler and his murderous regime. Worldwide boycotts ensued following the Nazi regime's ascension to power. As soon as the anti-Semitic programs of the new government became apparent, Jews everywhere began boycotts against Germany, its products, and its services. While it is difficult to understand how Jews could deal with the Nazi regime, the end result may have been to save many.

A flood of German-Jewish refugees poured out of the Third Reich as soon as it became apparent that five long years of Hitler's anti-Jewish election demagoguery were going to be put into practise when he rose to power. It was not just rhetoric—actual laws were being passed, and people were beaten on the streets of highly civilised Germany. The reaction of worldwide Jewry to these outrages coalesced in the strongest of the Jewish organizations, the Zionist movement.

In pre-World War II Germany, most Jews were not Zionist and overwhelming numbers of Jews in Germany were patriotic and loved their fatherland. Indeed, despite the impending horrors that seemed to be looming over them, most German Jews simply did not want to leave their country, and of all the possible destinations Palestine was the least desirable. It was hot and underdeveloped, especially for the middle-class assimilated Jews of Germany. Few of these German Jews had any Zionist leanings. Nevertheless it proved to be a place of salvation for tens of thousands of German Jews.

On July 13, 1933, Zionist leaders met with Nazi representatives on Wilhelmstrasse Street, a block of German government buildings in central Berlin. Together they began to negotiate a secret agreement whereby the assets of German Jewry would be transferred to Jewish Palestine. It would be a complicated transaction involving vast sums of money, property, and goods as well as foreign currency.

Tremendous opposition was engendered from the worldwide Jewish community. Many Jews, especially those among the right-wing Zionists, wanted to continue the boycott of German goods and services. It was felt that the boycott was hurting Germany economically. In fact this sense of economic pressure on Germany was correct, since the boycott was working Hitler and his minions were more than willing to negotiate with Jews.

The Eighteenth Zionist Congress opened in Prague, Czechoslovakia, on August 17, 1933. The Havara, or Transfer, Agreement was one of the most contentious items on the agenda. Finally the *New York Times* announced on Tuesday, August 29, that a barter arrangement between the Jews of Palestine and the German government had been achieved. Millions of dollars worth of Jaffa oranges would be exchanged for German industrial machinery. In addition, the Havara Agreement allowed German Jews to transfer their personal assets to Palestine in exchange for German goods, which would be purchased there. In the end the Congress voted for the Transfer Agreement.

The German government further indicated its readiness to allow German Jews to emigrate with cash in Reich marks and goods produced in Germany. This indicates that at this point, in 1933, the Nazis simply wanted to get rid of the Jews. At this point extermination of the Jews was simply not in the Nazi operational manual. If only the Jews had somewhere to go. In just three short years, the gates of Palestine would be virtually shut to Jewish immigration and the Jews of Europe would be trapped. The British blockade ensured that millions would perish in the fires of Auschwitz, Treblinka, Sobibor, and other places once the Nazis had decided on their extermination policies.

A German-Jewish family by the name of Mecklenberg immigrated legally to British Mandate Palestine in 1935, making use of the Havara Agreement. The father described himself as a Zionist-Progressive from Hamburg, Germany. Mr. Mecklenberg was religious and was also an accomplished physician. Following Hitler's rise to power in 1933, he had no longer been able to practice medicine in Germany because of anti-Jewish laws. Using the Havara Agreement's transfer laws, the Mecklenberg family was able to send a large portion of their wealth from Germany to Palestine. The son, John, described the family as having sufficient goods, two family cars and even a motorcycle in a fine home in what is now Hertzilya, Israel. They had a two-bedroom home in what would now be termed an affluent suburb in Israel. The older Mecklenberg opened a medical practice, which was one of the first institutions to feature X-rays. His practice was a huge success. In a scenario that was repeated Mecklenberg, the physician did not subscribe to Kupat Holim, the Histadruts' hospital insurance scheme, and was unable to secure a hospital position. This was because Mecklenberg was not a member of the Mapai Party, a left-wing labour party.

The eminent physician eventually became a deputy mayor of Hertzilya. In World War II he served in the British army and was promoted from captain to colonel. Mecklenberg served with distinction in the British Eighth Army at the key battle of El-Alamein and then helped win the War of Independence in the IDF. He continued to be a centrist politician with the Israeli Progressive Party.

Felicia Carmelly was born in Romania in 1931. She came from a traditional Jewish family that spoke four languages, including German, Russian, Romanian, and French. She remembers World War II beginning when she was ten years old and that it was illegal to have a radio at the time. She also remembers that Romania was a very anti-Semitic country. Felicia had been deported to Transnistria in October 1941 and had been liberated in March 1944. After experiencing more than a decade of Communism, Felicia realized that she did not like the doctrinaire equality and rigid laws of the Soviet Bloc's Communism. Instead, she substituted another ideology, something that suited her Jewish upbringing and tradition much more—Zionism. She went to a transit centre in Vienna and finally, convinced by Slichim (Zionist representatives), flew from Vienna to Tel Aviv. She had been strongly motivated by the first English book she had ever read—*Exodus*.

Felicia was tremendously energized by her new country and spent her first two years moving from Haifa to Tel Aviv before finally ending up in Rehovot. One concern that she experienced was the bias against Romanian Jews in Israel. Despite the large number of Romanians in Israel, it was felt that all Romanians were thieves.

Felicia recalled smuggling American money between family photographs on the train from Romania to Vienna. Another recollection was what appeared to be a very obese lady arguing vehemently with border guards about her diamond earrings. After a prolonged dispute, the very heavy lady gave up her earrings to the thieving border guards. Only later, after crossing the border, did anyone realise that the lady was actually svelte and slim. The diamond earrings were merely a ruse. The woman was wearing a very large corset packed with diamonds, silver, and gold, as well as American dollars, and was able to get them out of Romania by using her earrings as a distraction.

In the end Felicia Carmelly realized her one mistake about going to Israel. She had simply waited too long. The tremendous excitement that she experienced on her aliyah to Israel and the fervour that she had experienced when she lived there would have all been better if she had done it earlier. Perhaps, as she said, some ten years younger would have been easier.

While the focus of this book has been on illegal immigration, many more were able to come legally. Starting in the 1880s, there were four large waves of *aliyah*, mostly from Eastern Europe. Still, immigration in the period between 1933 and 1948 laid the foundation of the state, with the large German-Jewish influx made possible by the Havara Agreement being a key element in making the state of Israel possible. In addition, many ardent Zionists, such as Miriam Beckerman, came from established places like Canada and America. They left comfortable surroundings where anti-Semitism was minimal to help build a country in difficult times. Others, like Ben Miller, were able to get precious immigration certificates and flee hotbeds of anti-Semitism. These legal immigrants overcame seemingly insurmountable difficulties to establish lives in Israel.

CHAPTER 12

The Jews Who Served in the British Army and Police of Palestine

Even before World War II there was a substantial Jewish presence in the British police and armed forces in Palestine. As the war unfolded, large numbers of Jews joined the British military forces and eventually, late in the war, a specific Jewish brigade was formed, mainly at the urging of Winston Churchill. The Jews in the Palestinian police forces were supervised by British officers and made important contributions. The Arabs saw the British police and armed forces in a completely different light. They were resentful of the British supervision and always were paranoid about the Jewish presence. In addition, they saw the Germans during the war as their natural allies. The Arabs felt that Rommel and his Panzer units would eventually drive out the British and get rid of the Jews once and for all. Few Palestinian Arabs joined the British forces, and when they did, they usually accepted the monetary bonuses and quickly disappeared.

It is ironic, and not properly recognized, that while tens of thousands of Jewish servicemen recruited from Palestine served with distinction in the British Armed Forces, the Arabs stressed their loyalty to the Nazis. The Grand Mufti of Jerusalem, Mohammad Amin Al-Husanyi, took up residence in Berlin for most of the war and received the following telegram from Reichsfuhrer SS Heinrich Himmler on November 3, 1943. As head of the SS Himler was responsible for much of the implementation of the Holocaust:

The National Socialist movement of Greater Germany had since its inception inscribed upon its flag the fight against world Jewry. It has therefore followed with particular sympathy the struggle of freedom-loving Arabs especially in Palestine against Jewish interlopers. In the recognition of this enemy and of the common struggle against it lies the firm foundation of the natural alliance that exists between the National Socialist Greater Germany and the freedom-loving Muslims of the world. In this spirit I am sending you on the anniversary of the infamous Balfour Declaration my hearty greetings and wishes for the successful pursuit of your struggle until the final victory.

Ben Miller, a droll little man, described his experiences as a Jewish police officer in the mid-1930s. Somehow he had acquired a precious immigration certificate and successfully and legally made his way from Poland to British Mandate Palestine in 1935. Soon Ben found his way into the British-run police forces. He guarded Jewish settlements against the omnipresent Arab terrorism and generally enforced law and order in the Mandate. He was attired in the obligatory short pants, knee socks, and khaki shirt. While he enjoyed the job, he was appalled by the amount of corruption that always seemed to be present. The Mapai Party, the present-day Labour Party, seemed to have deep-rooted connections with the police forces and participated to some degree in the bribery. Miller became fed up with the bribery and eventually quit the police force. Nevertheless Ben Miller stayed on in Israel to fight heroically in the Israeli Army Zahal in the War of Independence in 1948.

Arie Lewin described his family as a family of warriors going back several generations. His father, at age twenty-one, joined the nascent Zionist movement in Germany. When Hitler came to power even the Lewins, middle-class Jewish-Germans were immediately affected. The family made a landmark decision to immigrate to Palestine. Soon preparations were started. As was the case with many families, the Lewins had to separate for the journey to Palestine.

Arie, then almost sixteen years of age, managed to get a legal immigration certificate and a one-way passport out of Germany to Palestine. The German authorities told him forcibly and in no uncertain terms that he would never be allowed back into Germany. He was allowed to take the equivalent of half a British pound with him in the form of a ten-mark gold coin. Perplexed, he hid the invaluable coin initially in his shoe. Then he realized on reflection that the Gestapo, the Nazi police force, would most probably search his shoes. Before inspection while on a train he hid the coin inside his belt buckle seam. As he correctly foresaw, his shoes were searched by the police but not his belt buckle. Decades later he still has the same ten-mark gold coin.

Along with the rest of his youthful compatriots who had prepared for their *aliyah* in a Hachshara in Blankenzene, Arie embarked on his epic journey. He arrived by train at Trieste in the late spring of 1938. One night, the barely adolescent boys and girls boarded a ship called the *Galileah* and left for Palestine. After a five-day journey they arrived at a makeshift port in Tel Aviv. Haifa was not used because of security concerns. Arie described no gangplank but a system of ropes and ladders to clamber down the side of the ship to waiting rowboats.

On his first day in Palestine, the bus carrying Arie and his fellow immigrants was fired on by Arab marauders. Upon his arrival he was quickly installed in a kibbutz, picking oranges and clementines. His Hebrew was passable but impeded by a heavy German accent. His proficiency in German was to stand him in good stead later.

Arie experienced another attack by Arabs when they fired on the kibbutz. Although it was 1938 and the Arab revolt had largely been put down, the Palestinian Arabs simply would not accept the presence of so many Jews. The large numbers of German and Austrian Jews immigrating had spurred the initial stages of the revolt and discontent still simmered between the two parties.

Arie soon joined the Haganah and received extensive training. By 1940 and 1941 British forces were reeling in North Africa and Rommel was approaching Palestine. The Yishuv united behind the British and determined to resist the Nazis in every way possible. It was at this time that

Ben Gurion made his famous quote with respect to illegal immigration and the war, stating, "We will fight the war as if there were no white paper and the white paper as if there were no war." The white paper he referred to was the document concerning British restrictions on Jewish immigration.

Arie's parents were amongst the last group of Jews to escape Nazi Germany. They made their way with many others in small vessels down the Danube. They travelled through Austria, Hungary, and Bulgaria before finally arriving at the Black Sea. These were some of the people who boarded the three renamed Greek ships, the *Milos*, *Pacific*, and *Atlantic*. Eventually Arie's parents were transferred to the *Patria*, but they survived the explosion and went on to be interned at Atlit. It was here that Arie visited his parents and talked to them through the heavy barbed wire. By this time he had joined the British army and his parents were shocked to see him in uniform. His mother was an excellent Hebrew teacher and thus was considered by British officials as a special security risk. She was interned by the British at Atlit for a very long several months.

In 1942 the British formed a strong bond with the Haganah-trained forces and hoped to train them to repel the approaching Rommel. British officers noted the excellent German language skills of Arie and decided to utilize them. He was initially given a British uniform and British identification documents under his real name. Eventually he was transformed into a Wehrmacht corporal named Rudolf Ludwig Lein, put into a German uniform, and placed into a transport of German prisoners of war moving across Egypt.

Arie's mission was to penetrate the German POW group and discover any of their plans for escape. Although the German prisoners were housed in tents, the food was tolerable and the conditions acceptable. Arie as well as another secret British operative in the prison camp found three high-ranking German officers who were going to orchestrate an escape attempt. Most German POWs were not interested in escape, as they realized the war was being lost and that escape was almost impossible considering the vast distances to German held territory.

Soon the British officers and high command decided to jail the German officers in a more secure setting. At this point Arie's true identity was revealed, along with that of the other British operative. The two British spies were given back their identity along with proper British uniforms. Properly armed, they were placed in a vehicle to guard the three German officers. The group was to make its way across the desert to a British base at Alexandria, Egypt. En route to the Alexandria base, one of the German officers jumped off the transport and tried to escape. He was brought down by a hail of gunfire and died. The German officer was left by the side of the road. Lewin and his partner transported the remaining two Germans to the British base. They were met by British intelligence officers and received numerous citations for their bravery and good work. Arie Lewin's tale of bravery, while extraordinary, was typical of the devotion of the Jewish members of the British armed forces in the area.

Other Jews wanted to form a Jewish army to save the Jewish people of Europe. An Abraham Cohen was interviewed in an article in the December 1942 issue of *Stars and Stripes*, an American armed forces magazine. They probably picked him as a typical Jew who had come to America. Although he had been born in Lodz, Poland, he had made his way to America before the war. He was then asked for his name and his place of birth.

"Abraham Cohen. Lodz, Poland."

"Where is your home?"

"I have no home."

"Parents?"

"All murdered. Brother and sisters disappeared. I may have one brother still alive."

This illustrates the lack of knowledge and comprehension regarding the Holocaust by the participants, even during the war.

Cohen further described going to the Committee for a Jewish Army. This was held at the St. Moritz Hotel in New York City in August 1942. The advertisement for the Jewish army contained the information that it was free admission but also had air conditioning, necessary in New York City in August. Abraham Cohen eventually found his way to the Irgun, the right-wing revisionist army, which ended up fighting the British in Palestine in the immediate postwar years.

Mickey Kestenbaum was another Jewish patriot who joined the British-armed forces in the Middle East. Mickey came from an ultra-Orthodox environment in Hungary but over the course of his life managed to acquire fluency in five different languages. A devout Talmudic scholar as a young man, Kestenbaum escaped Czechoslovakia in January 1944 and eventually found his way via train to Palestine. To the amazement of everyone, Mickey acquired the precious immigration certificate worth 2,000 American dollars, as well as all the relevant visas. He held exit visas to Syria, Bulgaria, and Yugoslavia, as well as a Turkish visa, which would enable him to make the final overland connections to Palestine.

Unlike many of the other journeys that have been described, Mickey was going not by sea but over land to Palestine. Mr. Krauss, a member of the Jewish agency that had to interview Mickey, was flabbergasted that Kestenbaum had managed to acquire the invaluable Turkish visa. Kestenbaum related the story that his brother had had a sexual liaison with a key Turkish contact and persuaded her to grant Mickey the Turkish visa. In January 1944, Mickey had met his brother in Belgrade, Yugoslavia, acquired the visa, and made his way by train through Bulgaria to Istanbul and Ankara in Turkey before continuing on through Syria and Lebanon and finally arriving in Palestine.

After listening to a speech by Moshe Shertok at Hebrew University, Mickey was hooked on Zionism and joined the British army, along with nine other Jewish boys. After crossing the Suez Canal, they saw some action in what is today Libya. Following Rommel's collapse and defeat in North Africa, this brave Jewish group joined the British Eighth Army in Italy. Mickey remarked that he was able to use a language of antiquity, Latin, to communicate in Italy.

After the war ended Mickey found his way back to Israel. Now speaking Hebrew fluently, he was invited to join the Stern gang. This was the extreme right-wing group that would stop at nothing to defeat the British, including cooperation with the Nazis. Kestenbaum resisted the entreaties of the Stern gang and instead joined the more mainstream Haganah. He fought in the Israeli War of Independence and used his language and other skills to help with the Haganah's intelligence section. Mickey Kestenbaum is another example of a brave young man who devoted his young life to helping the Jewish cause in Palestine.

Rudi Landecker wrote his memoir based on a series of letters to his mother while he was in the British army. His first notes concerned his purchase of the mandatory knee-length khaki socks that all British officers wore. The socks were six shillings, about $1.50 then, and purchased in the Bata shoe store in Kenya. Rudi passed through Aden in Yemen and while frequenting a shop noticed the familiar blue and white Keren Khaymet donation box. He realized that the store owners in Aden were Jewish and were not afraid to display their Jewishness. It is doubtful that a similar Jewish display would be countenanced in today's Aden. The proprietor told him that there were six thousand Mizrachi or Arab Jews in Aden at the time.

After passing through Egypt, Rudi Landecker entered Palestine through Gaza. He noticed immediately the contrasting scenery between Egypt and Palestine. Rudi described orange groves and fields richly cultivated with vegetables and fruit in Palestine, as opposed to the arid wasteland of Egypt. The influence of the Jewish pioneers with their superior irrigation and cultivation techniques was being felt already, even prior to the independence of Israel. He found British Mandate Palestine neat and tidy, with even the Arab villages having higher living standards than their Egyptian Arab counterparts. Rudi arrived in Jerusalem on May 14, 1945, barely a week after the war had ended. He found thousands of German and Austrian Jewish refugees in Jerusalem, each largely living within their own separate social circles.

Prices were inordinately high because of the shortage of raw materials, but Rudi was amazed at the quality of the goods and especially, as he put it, the "snappy styles." The socialist and egalitarian influence of the eventual Israeli state was well in evidence as many prices were controlled, including the freezing of apartment rents.

Rudi went on tour to Bethlehem, which was much more Christianized than the Bethlehem of the late twentieth and early twenty-first century. A sizeable Christian emigration has taken place in the fifty years since the Balfour Declaration. Landecker then went on to see for the first time the

Wailing, or Western Wall, the last surviving remnant of the second Jewish temple. He was struck by attempts at commercialization. It should be noted that under the British Mandate Jews had free and easy access to the wall, or Kotel. After Israel became a state in 1948, the old city of Jerusalem was lost to the Jordanians in the War of Independence. Jewish passage to the wall was forbidden from 1948 to 1967. In 1967, during the Six-Day War, the old city of Jerusalem was captured by the Israelis and Jewish access to the wall was restored.

Landecker met with several Zionists who felt that it would take more than twenty years to make any progress towards a viable country. The dire predictions made by the Zionists were wrong. By 1965, Israel had beaten the Arabs decisively in two major conflicts, in 1948 and 1956, and was in position to inflict on the Arabs the catastrophic defeat of 1967.

Landecker provided many interesting insights on the Yishuv of 1945, the Jewish settlement in British Mandate Palestine. He was thoroughly impressed by Tel Aviv, which he viewed as a modern city. After completing his exhaustive tour of Palestine, Rudi concluded that it was a poor country aspiring for more. Years later, another native born Israeli described the country as a terribly poor country with very rich people.

Victor Sefton was transferred from Europe to Palestine in October 1945. He was in the elite British Sixth Airborne division and was sent with the Red Beret paratroopers to "fight the Jews." Victor had spent time slogging up the Italian peninsula and had finally arrived in sunny Palestine. He was impressed with his barracks in Hadera. Every room had a sack of Jaffa oranges in it, which the soldiers were encouraged to eat. The oranges could not be exported because of the wartime conditions, but the trees needed to be cleared to make room for new crops, hence the unlimited supply of free oranges to be eaten.

Sefton felt that his impressions of Palestine were strongly coloured by his firm Jewish identity. He was impressed by the farming and modern irrigation methods. He was also fascinated by the three languages that permeated mandate Palestine: Hebrew, English, and Arabic. Victor enjoyed a good faculty with Yiddish, which enabled him to converse with the large influx of Holocaust survivors, most of whom were from Eastern Europe.

Sefton was constantly embarrassed, because he was able to understand whatever was said about him and other British officers regardless of which of the four languages was being used.

Victor also had occasion to meet rising luminaries that were to be future stars in the Israeli political scene. Vivian Herzog was an army captain in the British army and rose to be a general in the future Israeli army. Herzog climbed the political ladder to become a distinguished president of Israel. Sefton felt that Herzog was a charming man who deserved his future political status. Victor also met Teddy Kolleck, who became the celebrated and long-serving mayor of Jerusalem.

Rationing in wartime Palestine was not as severe as rationing in England and certainly not comparable to rationing in Nazi-occupied Europe. Sefton was amazed when he arrived in Palestine to find both razors and soap in amply supply. He also was pleased with the skills of the Jewish Palestinian population, as he and his army friends were finally able to easily get watches and cameras. From Victor's comments, the simple level of civilization in British Mandate Palestine far exceeded his expectations. Above all, Victor and his fellow British soldiers were amazed by the normalcy of Tel Aviv. Clearly the war never really struck Palestine. Although the Germans threatened, Rommel was stopped at El Alamein in 1942, and the devastation that struck so much of Europe never touched the British Mandate.

Sefton saw numerous Jewish girls presumably soliciting British officers and enlisted men on Hayarkon Street in Tel Aviv. He naturally assumed that they were prostitutes. It was only years later that Sefton learned that these encounters with British soldiers were to find ways to get both information and British ammunition for the Haganah.

Sometimes Sefton's perceptions did not ring true. He recalled a comedian at an outdoor night club in Haifa making euphoric comments about the July 1945 defeat of Winston Churchill in the British general election. It was naturally assumed that the labour government of Clement Atlee and his foreign minister Aneurin Bevan would be much more favourable to the Jews in Palestine. This was simply not true. From 1945 to 1948, the Atlee government opposed Jewish immigration and the drive for Jewish self-government in Palestine by all means possible. In fact, it can be said that the fight between the Jews and the British reached its apex in the three years between the end of the war in May 1945, Winston Churchill's defeat in the July 1945 general election, and Israeli independence in 1948.

The Jews of Palestine served with distinction, honour, and bravery in both the police and armed forces. They made a substantial contribution to the eventual defeat of the German forces in North Africa and then later fought in Italy. It was unfortunate that the British authorities did not allow Jewish units until late in the war and only after the urging of Winston Churchill. It also has to be recognized that the training and experience that the Jewish brigades and other Jewish soldiers received eventually made substantial contributions to the founding of the Israeli Defence Forces (IDF).

Adolf Hitler conferring with the Grand Mufti.

The Grand Mufti of Jerusalem shaking hands with
Heinrich Himmler of the SS.

A victorious General Erwin Rommel surrounded by British prisoners.

CHAPTER 13

Liberation from Nazi Occupied Europe

On January 25, 1995, the fiftieth anniversary commemoration of the liberation of Auschwitz was held. There was a dais filled with many dignitaries, amongst them Vice President Al Gore of the United States and President Vladimir Putin of Russia. Many grizzled veterans of the Russian army who had liberated Auschwitz came. In addition, numerous Holocaust survivors came to see and commemorate what they had survived. Amongst the Holocaust survivors was an Israeli woman, Mrs. Merka Shevach.

During the ceremony, Merka Shevach leapt to the podium and seized the microphone away from the assembled elites. Despite the biting cold and wind, she bared her arm and showed her Auschwitz number—the blue number tattoo forever emblazoned on her skin. She shouted out, "I was brought here as a child, they murdered my parents and family, they stole my name and identity and made me into a slave. It will never happen again, never! Now I have a name, a country, a president and an army, and my country, Israel. It will never happen again, never!"

In a sense, Mrs. Shevach's outburst symbolized the great transition of the Jewish people. The assembled dignitaries were clearly moved and sat in silence. Even the Russian war veterans who had liberated Auschwitz some fifty years before had tears dribbling down their cheeks.

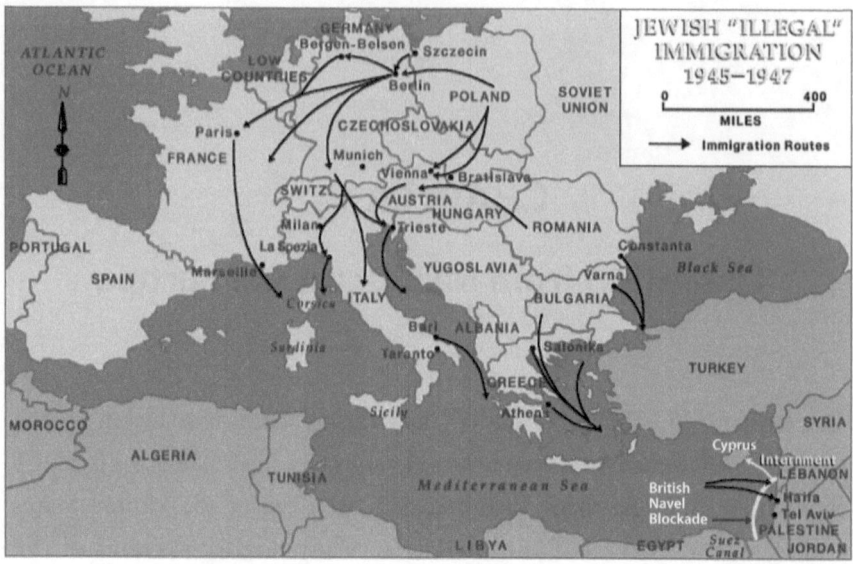

There were perhaps a dozen camps scattered throughout Europe, mainly in Poland, meant for extermination. Auschwitz was a dual-purpose camp, with Auschwitz-Birkenau being the extermination site and Auschwitz itself a slave labour facility. Auschwitz, only a few miles from Krakow, remains a key symbol, a paradigm for the horrors of the twentieth century. While the number of people murdered at Auschwitz can be estimated at approximately two million, other camps, such as Treblinka, which was the primary location used to murder Jews from Warsaw, exterminated perhaps 800,000 innocent people. If Auschwitz was a paradigm for the horrors of the twentieth century, then Bergen-Belsen, primarily a work camp and the place where Anne Frank died in the closing months of World War II, was the example of all that could go wrong in liberation.

Bergen-Belsen was liberated by the British army in 1945. The British were simply unprepared for the nightmare that confronted them. At the initial liberation an estimated ten thousand inmates were fed a diet with too much fat and died as a result. There were no adequate medical facilities to cope with the thousands of starving and dying prisoners of the Nazis.

British bulldozers dug huge pits and simply pushed mounds of dead into them. Nevertheless, from those horrors emerged the survivors, more than 300,000 of which would go to live in what eventually became Israel.

Henry Melnyk described his liberation from Bergen-Belsen. Henry, who was born in Lodz, Poland, saw a column of British tanks knocking down the gates and pouring into the camp. He could not believe his eyes as the German SS guards put on white armbands and raised white flags. British military police with red berets disarmed the Nazis. Henry fled down into the basement of a nearby German army base building. He fell into a pile of potatoes on which he immediately gorged himself. Then he stuffed as many potatoes as he could into his shirt. He heard shooting in the camp and somehow, as he put it, became Superman and flew out of the basement window of the incredibly congested quarters.

He stayed in hospital for two long weeks recovering from his starvation diet. Henry was then put in a displaced persons camp for a number of months. From there he made his way to Hanover, Germany, where he remained for two years and made connections with the Bricha.[17] After getting married in 1946, Melnyk described a torturous route on his journey to Palestine. Border guards were bribed and Jewish Brigade soldiers who discarded their official British uniforms all helped with his passage to what was then Palestine. He was in Aachen and then Dusseldorf, Germany, before he finally arrived in France and literally missed the boat and couldn't get on to the *Exodus 1947*. Eventually Melynk made his way to Marseille, where he was put on a Romanian ship ironically named the *Transylvania*. It was a small ship which stayed in Naples, Italy, for a week. Finally he was disembarked in Haifa, where he was looked after by the Jewish Agency. He had been trained by the Organization for Rehabilitation and Training (ORT) in Germany and went on to be a valuable electrician in the new Israeli army.

Another survivor described Bergen-Belsen as a symbol of man's inhumanity to man. He painted a picture of thousands of living skeletons dying from torture, starvation, and epidemic diseases. He said that

---

[17] The Flight organized by the Jewish Agency.

nothing could describe the horrendous, inhumane cruelty that had been visited on the inmates. British jeeps armed with loudspeakers penetrated the camp and repeated the announcement, "Hello, hello you are free! We are British soldiers and we came to liberate you." One of the liberators was Brigadier General Glyn Hughes, who later enforced the British Mandate immigration restrictions against these same Holocaust survivors.

That same survivor's memories consisted of the horror of remembering ten thousand unburied dead and thirteen thousand more that died after liberation. The Swedish government and the Red Cross accepted some six thousand patients for recuperation under UNRRA (United Nations Relief and Rehabilitation Association) auspices. The British authorities were constantly worried that the survivors would eventually go to Palestine and break their blockade. Many survivors complained that the British were more concerned about Palestinian Jewish immigration then helping the unfortunate survivors of the camps.

A Bergen-Belsen Jewish committee was formed and aid was received from the Joint, another Jewish relief agency from Britain as well as the World Jewish Congress.

A particularly searing memory for the survivors was meeting with soldiers of the Jewish Brigade and other volunteers from Palestine. To see Jewish soldiers with their Star of David shoulder patches was a tremendous moment for all of those that had survived.

The liberation of Bergen-Belsen was one of many such episodes that resonated with the tens of thousands of survivors in many other camps. Some, such as Treblinka and Sobibor, had almost no surviving inmates, but others, such as Auschwitz, had many. In addition to those surviving the concentration camps there were many hidden in forests, caves, and bunkers. The war was over and the Sher Ha-Palit, the remnants of the Jews who survived in Europe, began to emerge from their hiding places. While most of the Nazi slaughter had taken place in Eastern Europe in countries such as Poland, the Ukraine, Russia, and Belarus, many had hid themselves in Nazi-occupied Western European countries like France and Holland.

One family of Polish Jews had immigrated to France before the war. Those Jews in France who were not French citizens were a particular target for the Nazis and their collaborators, the Vichy government. The Shene family had secreted their two daughters and a son in three convents scattered across Vichy France. Nuns protected the three children as if they were Catholics. The three children survived the war to eventually immigrate to Palestine, but their parents were murdered at Auschwitz. These were the three orphans who somehow dragged the little Hassidic boy aboard a ship.

Moshe Bitterman returned to his family owned inn in the south of Poland. He came from a large extended family of eleven. Eventually through the horrible course of the war all of Moshe's family, his two brothers, four sisters, and parents perished, all at the hands of the Nazis. Even at the very end of conflagration, Moshe still did not know the fate of all his family members. As he climbed up the steps to the former family inn, a belligerent Pole who had taken possession of the property cried out, "I thought you were burnt up like the rest of the Jews. All of you Jews should have been killed!" Moshe Bitterman fled, never to return.

Molly Sternberg, hiding in a dugout hidden in a forest, emerged when Russian soldiers approached. The Sternberg family had been aided and sustained by Polish farmers. Nevertheless as the war reached its climax food became harder and harder to get. Molly's initial postwar memory was a Russian soldier digging in the ground and finding a prize possession to eat—a potato!

A transformational moment for Polish Jews was the Kielce Pogrom in July 1946. Some elements of the Jews who had been in the resistance against the Nazis still carried firearms. The Jewish militia and other Jewish agencies established a base at 7 Palanty Street in Kielce, Poland. Right-wing Polish elements bitterly resented the Jewish armed presence. Soon rumours were spread that a Christian child had been murdered by the Jews and that his blood was being used for Jewish rituals. It is hard to accept today that even in the modern era, in the twentieth century, a medieval tale of blood libel would be believed, but it was.

Soon right wing Poles attacked 7 Palanty Street. The few Jews bearing arms were killed, and many others were simply thrown out of windows. Considerable numbers were killed and the rioting was only put down when the regular Polish army arrived. Dozens of other riots, pogroms, and massacres were sparked across Poland by the Kielce pogrom. Rumours persist until today that the original killings were perpetuated by a Soviet NKVD provocateur. The Russian motive was to instigate a mass movement of the Polish Jews and make trouble for the British Mandate with more Jewish immigration.

Whatever the initial cause the movement of Polish Jews out of Poland received a tremendous impetuous. Prewar Poland in 1939 was the home to some 3.5 million Jewish people. After the Holocaust and World War II, perhaps 10 percent of the original population, about 350,000 Jews, had survived. Within a few months of the Kielce pogrom, only 50,000 Jews remained in Poland. By 1967, on the eve of the Six-Day War between Israel and its Arab neighbours, there were about 25,000 Jewish people in Poland. Following Israel's dramatic victories in the Six-Day War, most of the surviving small Jewish population were expelled or had fled. By the 1970s, some 5,000-10,000 Jews, mostly aged, constituted the only remnants of the prewar 3.5 million Polish Jews. As one prominent sociologist Alexander Herz put it, "All the Shabbat candles had gone out."

Hundreds of thousands of Holocaust survivors began to coalesce in displaced persons camps. These were established mainly in the American-and British-occupied zones of Germany. Many survivors pondered whether to go east or west. Molly Sternberg recounted an encounter on a train in Eastern Europe. Many of these people had been liberated by Soviet troops or had been saved by Russian soldiers. Molly Sternberg sat opposite a Soviet major, a Jew on a train in Poland. "Where should I go, east or west?" was the question. The Jewish major pondered a moment, making sure that no one overheard him.

"You are a Jew! Go to the west."

Molly and her husband Abel listened to the advice and after spending time in displaced persons camps in Germany eventually found their way to Canada.

In the immediate postwar immigration period, restrictions were severe, especially in North America. Those who badly wanted to get into the so-called Golden Medina States of the United States and Canada were unable to do so. In addition, the Jewish Agency and other Zionist mainline organizations heavily promoted immigration to British Mandate Palestine, but the British authorities stuck to their tiny immigration quotas of fifteen hundred people per month. King Ibn-Saud, ruler of Saudi Arabia, met with President Roosevelt and commented that the Arabs were terrified of Nazi-like Zionists who were going to massacre the Arab Palestinians. On October 19, 1945, President Truman requested Clement Atlee, the British prime minister, to immediately admit 100,000 Jews from their displaced persons camps into Palestine. He was refused. As a result tens of thousands were confined in the displaced persons camps. Although no one was killed and there was virtually no violence, the camps were barely an improvement over their Nazi predecessors. Barbed wire, stockades, watchtowers with searchlights, armed guards, and dogs comprised the perimeters of the camps.

Finally on May 1, 1946, an Anglo-American committee reported that the land sales restrictions would be lifted and that the 100,000 refugees languishing in the concentration-like camps of Europe would be admitted to Palestine. The entire front page of the *Palestine Post* was filled with the report of the committee. It should be considered that tremendous world sympathy was being engendered for the Holocaust survivors.

President Harry Truman sent Benjamin Harrison with a delegation to inspect the camps. Harrison submitted a report to President Truman which resulted in another strong request to the British government of Clement Atlee to immediately allow 100,000 Jewish refugees to be admitted to Palestine. The American note was refused and the refugees continued to languish in squalid conditions.

David Ben-Gurion, the future Israeli prime minister, toured the camps. Ben-Gurion despised the Yiddish that most survivors spoke. He was a firm advocate of Hebrew, which he correctly foresaw as the future language of Israel. Considering that there are immigrants and refugees from over a hundred different countries residing in the state of Israel, the Hebrew language became one of the main unifiers of the country.

Prior to May 1948 there was no state of Israel and many still did not appreciate the status of Hebrew and most did not speak it. Ben-Gurion visited the camps and addressed the beleaguered throngs in Hebrew. He would not take questions in Yiddish, which he termed a grating language. There was considerable friction over the language issue. In addition, many survivors found Ben-Gurion a poor speaker. He certainly could never have been termed a charismatic speaker. Indeed, one survivor simply described him "as not a very exciting speaker." Many viewed the future prime minister of Israel as a man who did not care enough about the survivors.

Indeed, the Yishuv, the Jewish quasi-state under the British Mandate, has been accused of not doing enough to save Jews during the war. This is clearly an unfair comment for many reasons. Firstly, the Yishuv had no power. It was subservient to the British authorities, who controlled all access. The Mandate had set strict immigration quotas which they rigorously enforced and never relaxed despite the slaughter of the Jews in the Holocaust.

Not only did the British refuse to allow refugees into Palestine, but they also shot at them to prevent them from entering. The first shots of the war on September 1, 1939, were fired at the illegal immigration ship the *Tiger Hill* off the shores of Tel-Aviv. Many other illegal immigrant ships were also fired upon during the course of the war. As well, other ships were sunk directly because of British actions. What could the Yishuv have done in defiance of the British policies?

There had been two major exchanges of Palestinian Jewish nationals who had held British passports and were working in Poland before the war with German citizens residing in Palestine. The Jewish groups brought back horror stories of occupied Poland. These accounts were early in the war and prior to the implementation of the Nazi mass killings of Jews which effectively started in June 1941 with the German invasion of Soviet Russia. Over and over the same conclusions can be reached. What we know does not necessarily equate to comprehension.

"Knowledge is not comprehension" is an effective statement about the deciphering of the lack of reaction to the Holocaust. Who could conceive that a modern nation like Germany could exterminate millions of innocent people? It was clearly incomprehensible to almost all until it was too late.

The Yishuv had no power and no means to intervene in the German genocide. A Jewish Brigade was formed only in the later years of the war, in 1944. By then it was far too late to help the masses of Polish and other East European Jews. To indict the Jews of Palestine for the lack of aid to their fellows Jews in Europe simply runs against the flow of history.

Alex Eisen, an Austrian Jew born in Vienna, had another tale of his liberation and journey to Israel. Alexander's father was a prominent cantor in a large synagogue in Vienna. Alexander's family was upper-middle-class Austrian Jewish. After experiencing the German Anschluss of Austria in March 1938 they decided to go to Budapest, Hungary, even though none of them spoke Hungarian and they had little money. The father was arrested and spent time in jail in Budapest, while Alex, by a torturous route, found his way to France. After Alex spent eight months in a DP camp in France he became completely Zionistic. Eventually he was reunited with his family in Israel.

Another survivor described the days in the DP camps as very long, tedious, and demoralizing. "Why do they want to bring children into this horrible environment?" was an oft-asked question. Yet the facts show that in the first few years immediately following liberation the survivor birth rates exploded. After undergoing the horrendous experiences of the Holocaust, the Jewish people proved their resilience and showed Hitler and the Nazis that they didn't win.

The Bricha was the flight of Jews from Europe, mostly from Eastern Europe, organized by the Jewish Agency and other Zionist groups to enable Jews to immigrate to Palestine. The British had stuck to their immigration policies and quotas. Only the precious fifteen hundred immigration certificates would be issued regardless of the deprivations of the Holocaust survivors. The refugees continued to languish in miserable conditions in the DP camps of postwar Europe.

As time went on, conditions improved somewhat, especially because of the efforts of the Benjamin Harrison investigation committee and pressure from the American government, led by President Harry Truman. The DPs in the camps began to develop a goal and a final destination—Palestine. As Deborah Dworkin and Robert Jan Van Pelt phrased it, it became a "debt to the dead, retribution toward the enemy and a duty to the living."

Immigration to Palestine developed into two basic streams. The first, the so-called A-immigrations consisted of those who had the valuable legal British certificates. The second stream was based in the Yishuv and called L'Aliyah Bet—B-immigration or illegal immigration, consisting of those with no certificates. The majority of the immigrants who went illegally and clandestinely began to regard it somewhat as an adventure but primarily as an idealistic duty.

These illegal immigrants defied the British and crossed by land through forests and mountains and then by boat. They staggered through snow and rain and finally arrived in any one of a number of Mediterranean ports in France and Italy. From there they embarked on decrepit and leaky boats to challenge the mighty British navy and run their blockade. Despite British efforts some 142,000 Jewish immigrants made it to Palestine in the post war period, about half illegally.

Passengers of the Wedgwood, the first of the American Aliyah Bet vessels

The Wedgewood—Jewish refugees approaching their homeland.

CHAPTER 14

Exodus 1947:
The Ship That Launched a Nation

By 1947, the British were at their wits' end in the British Mandate Palestine. Several events converged to put unrelenting pressure on the British. There had been the serious pogrom in Kielce, Poland, in which dozens had been killed. Prewar Poland had had a Jewish prewar population of some 3.5 million. Following the war, the survivors of the Holocaust, about 250,000-300,000, or some 10 percent of the original Polish-Jewish population, returned to their ancestral homeland from Soviet Russia. Spurred on by the Bricha almost 100,000 people left in the first postwar year.

The Kielce Pogrom was the final straw for most of the remnants of Polish Jewry. On July 4, 1946, following accusations that Jews were killing Polish babies and using their blood, a violent attack on the Jews of Kielce broke out. In addition, the Polish Cardinal August Hlond made inflammatory statements connecting the Jews to the unwanted Polish-Communist government. Some of the Polish Communist administrators were of Jewish origin. After these events, the Jews of Poland began to leave the country en masse. A dispatch in the *Palestinian Post* of July 17, 1946, reported that nine thousand Jews had fled Poland and up to twenty thousand more were expected to flee.

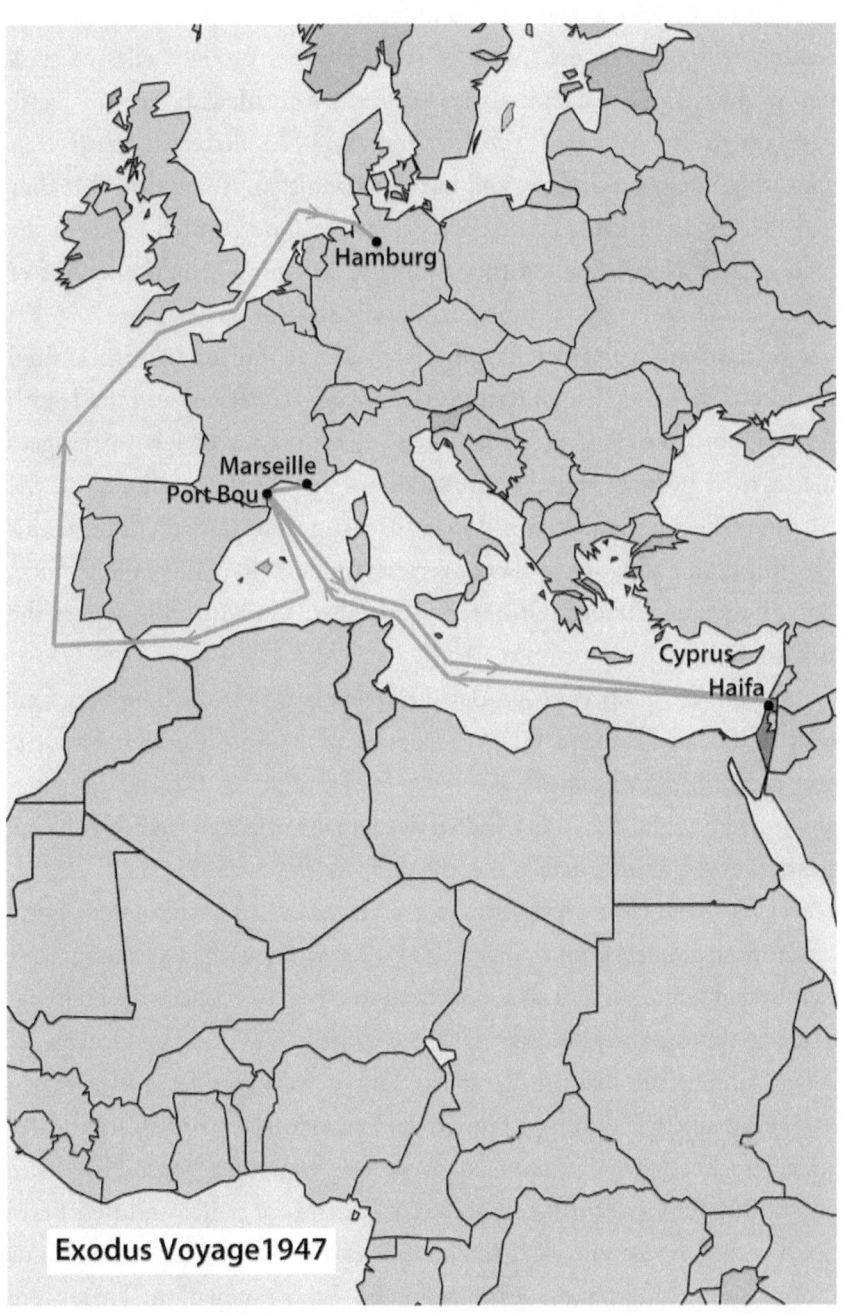

The Voyage of the Exodus

Reports from Austria on July 18, 1946, a scant two weeks after the murders of the Kielce pogrom, found more than five thousand Polish Jews seeking refuge in Vienna. Most of these refugees brought tales of stark terror. They described a nation-wide outbreak of anti-Jewish fury in Poland. A report in the *New York Times* of July 19, 1946, described the Jews as appearing in ragged clothing and in filthy condition. It was clear that they had fled for their lives. The report stated that most wanted to go to the "Holy Land"—Palestine. As they waited to get to the American Zone of occupied Germany they slept in corridors and rough shelters.

By mid-1946 the Bricha, or flight, was in full operation. United Nations Relief and Rehabilitation Association (UNRRA) and the Jewish Agency both provided aid. Many tens of thousands of Jewish refugees made their way to various ports along the northern shores of the Mediterranean to embark on ships to Palestine. At the same time as this vast migration of people were converging on ports like Marseille, France, Bari, Italy, and Piraeus, Greece, the so-called Jewish terror against the British was reaching a climax.

On July 22, 1946, the King David Hotel in Jerusalem was blown up. One wing of the hotel contained the headquarters of the British army in Palestine and the British government secretariat for Palestine. In the end casualties amounted to more than one hundred dead, many of whom were Jewish civil servants of the British. While the initial blame was put solely on the Irgun, years later it was clearly revealed that the Haganah had cooperated with the Irgun in planning the operation. It is also known now that warning phone calls were given to the British authorities and others to evacuate the building. The warning was not heeded, and the comment was made by General Sir Allan Cunningham that British officers did not take orders from Jews.

Following the bombing of the King David Hotel the British authorities sealed off Tel Aviv with more than twenty thousand troops. The entire city of 200,000 was cordoned off and thousands of police and Red Beret Sixth Airborne soldiers searched almost everyone. People were placed into groups comprising diverse segments of Tel Aviv's population. There were Orthodox Jews with their round hats and earlocks. There were elegant women with parasols and sundresses and other men and women in shorts.

All were searched thoroughly by the British. A curfew completely shut down the city until 5 a.m.

On Sunday, June 30, 1946, the British army seized the leaders of the Jewish Agency and arrested one thousand others. The British authorities had to respond to the ongoing attacks of the Haganah and the Irgun. A number of the leaders were interned, amongst them Golda Meir, who immediately went on a hunger strike. British officials clearly linked what they termed "Jewish terrorism" or "Zionist terrorism" to the Jewish Agency. American newspapers were filled with conflicting views on the situation in Palestine in 1946 following the King David Hotel bombing. While the Zionists in America seemed to support Jewish efforts in Palestine, anti-Zionist groups like the American Jewish Committee attacked Jewish leadership in British Mandate Palestine. The *New York Times* felt that the young Jewish element strongly supported action against the British.

Nevertheless, the bombing created a rift in the Jewish community. It stopped all cooperation between the Revisionists, comprised of the Lehi and the Irgun, and the mainstream Zionist military organization the Haganah. Indeed, David Ben-Gurion of the left wing led an all-out attack on the right-wing Irgun, turning them in to the British authorities. This attack of Jew upon Jew was called the Sezon.

The King David Hotel bombing was perhaps the culmination of a long series of attacks by Zionists of both the left and the right wing on the British. At this point in mid-1946, the British had over 100,000 soldiers trying to pacify 600,000 Jews in Palestine. In August 1946, less than a month after the King David Hotel bombing, British Mandate authorities shut down all immigration. None were to be landed and all illegal immigrants were being sent to Cyprus pending decisions on their future. It is in this context that plans began to be made for a giant refugee ship to be prepared to break the British blockade.

Some forty illegal ships had attempted to run the British blockade in the postwar period from May 1945 to July 1947. An overwhelming number of these ships initially were sent by the revisionists, with a few sent by the Mossad and some privately As the postwar struggle between the British and the Jews in Palestine more and more of the ships were sent by the mainstream Zionist movement. There was a tremendous split in Zionist ranks about how strongly to oppose the British. Some of these forty ships were shipwrecked, some sank, one or two caught fire, and one experienced an epidemic. One ship, during the war, the *Mefkure*, attacked by either the Germans or the Russians, was torpedoed and the survivors were machine gunned in the water. About 345 passengers died in the attack.

Who were these Jews that participated in this epic struggle? They were without a doubt most intensely idealistic. They were the same young people who led the resistance against the Nazis. They were similar to people like Tuvia Bielski, of Defiance fame. They were like Mordechai Awalewicz of the Warsaw Ghetto Uprising. They were like Hannah Senesch and Abba Kovno, who were poets and idealists. They were Jews and they were Zionists.

While it was mainly the revisionists who launched the first refugee ships, as the bitterness towards the British grew worse, the mainstream movements took over. The passengers were mostly Holocaust survivors with a few highly motivated American Zionists. By 1947, knowledge of the Shoah was quite definite, but even then, comprehension of that horrible tragedy was not yet complete. It was not something that survivors talked about. The first books about the Shoah were only written in 1960, after the trial of Adolf Eichmann.

On February 25, 1947, the Palmach, the elite military wing of the Haganah, appointed Ike Aronowicz as the captain of the ship the *President Warfield*, renamed *Exodus 1947*, and it sailed from Baltimore across the Atlantic to a French port in the Mediterranean.

The crew of the *Exodus 1947* was composed mostly of Jews, although there was a Christian clergyman aboard named Reverend John Gravel, an ordained Methodist minister. It was clear that there was a deep division between the American and Palestinian Jews on the *Exodus 1947*. Amongst the American Jews on board was the captain, Bill Ash, the first mate, Bernard Marks from Cincinnati, who had been in the Eighty-Second Airborne, another mate, William Bernstein, who was twenty-three years old, Murray Arnoff, an aggressive New Yorker, Nat Nadler, a mechanic, "Big" Bill Millman, a former boxing champion, and Dave Millman, who, while not related to Big Bill, was the cook. Other American members of the crew included Harold Leidner, a college graduate, David Malovsky, an electrician, Abe Lipschitz, the pharmacist mate (a sort of paramedic), Leonard Sklar, and Frank Levine. Most of these Americans were very practical and hardworking but they did not possess the idealism of the Palestinian Jews from the Haganah. There were constant battles, verbal and otherwise, between members of the Haganah and the Americans. With their fervent dedication and idealism, the Palestinian Jews could not accept the easy going ways of the American Jews.

Moshe Bitterman, a Polish Jew and the only survivor of a family of eleven, found himself in Weiden, Bavaria in 1946. He spent his time thinking about his future life. When he had gone back to his family home in Southern Poland he was greeted by taunts such as, "Why wasn't he burnt up like the rest?" Moshe wandered through the countryside and felt that he was a homeless person with no nation to call home. There was one place that Moshe focused on—the future state of Israel.

To resolve his deep conviction he went to an Orthodox kibbutz run by Agudath, Israel. These Kibbutzim were part of Hahschra, or preparation for a life in the future Israel. There had been many such kibbutzim in prewar Poland, and there were now many all over liberated Europe.

Moshe learned about farming which, as he explained, was not easy as most of the teenaged survivors came from urban areas. There were many classes, Hebrew lessons, and endless preparation.

Eventually five thousand mostly young people were assembled and sent by train to Marseille, France. They were then taken in trucks under the cover of darkness to nearby Sète, France. Then Moshe saw the ship, which was really a wooden boat. Moshe immediately surmised that the boat leaked. Moshe also knew that British Intelligence was watching the boat, at this point still called the *President Warfield*. As soon as the *President Warfield* sailed a huge blue and white banner was unveiled renaming the vessel *Exodus 1947*.

The *President Warfield* was what was called a packet steamer. It had carried freight between Baltimore, Maryland and Norfolk, Virginia, from 1928 to 1942. Then it was given to the British Ministry of War as a troop carrier. It had almost been torpedoed by Germans. It gave illustrious service on D-Day, when it was a holding station for troops ashore. In 1946 it was sold by the War Supplies Administration of the United States to the Potomac Wrecking Company, which was a front for the Haganah.

Bitterman described the interior of the ship as having shelves for sleeping, about four shelves high, the entire length of the boat with very narrow spaces to walk between the shelves. Astutely, Bitterman realized that the ship was little more than a ferry boat with bunk shelves. He wondered aloud how it had crossed the Atlantic and even more importantly how the newly named *Exodus 1947* would be able to cross the Mediterranean.

The embarkation, while highly organized, was difficult. Bitterman described boarding the ship along a plank two feet wide carrying his knapsack. He was allowed to bring about 10 kilos (22 lbs) on board with him and had to pack the rest in suitcases which would be shipped later in another boat. These suitcases never arrived, and Bitterman never saw the rest of his meagre possessions. In a wise move he had kept his family pictures, photographs of his ten family members destroyed in the Holocaust, on his person.

Exodus 1947 left Sète, France on July 11, 1947, with 4,500 passengers and had almost reached Palestine on July 18, 1947. The voyage to Palestine lasted eight days. Food and water were scarce and showers were nonexistent. Line-ups for washroom facilities were horrendous. Everywhere one went on the ship one experienced the terrible overcrowding. Despite these miserable conditions the passengers exhibited tremendous resilience. Most, if not all, were Holocaust survivors.

Regarding the food, Bitterman had a wonderful line. He had described food in the concentration camps and scavenging for potato peels. Years later, as Moshe described it, the same potato peels became delicacies at Bar/Bat Mitzvah cocktail parties.

The ship was intercepted in international waters by the British Cruiser *Ajax*, which had become famous for its participation in the *Graf Spee* (a famous German battleship) attack. Several additional destroyers that Bitterman had spotted shadowing the *Exodus 1947* from the beginning of the journey also moved to intercept the ship. The British used loudspeakers to hail the ship. Just outside of Haifa the British attack began. At that point more than four thousand Jews had assembled on deck to sing Hatikvah.

Forty kilometres (25 miles) from the coast, in international waters, it was rammed by two British destroyers, the *Chieftain* and the *Ajax,* and the British attempted to board the *Exodus 1947.* The passengers were determined to resist. Wire mesh had been put up to prevent the British from boarding and oil had been spilt on the decks to make boarding doubly difficult. As well, steam and water hoses were deployed to resist the British.

In the ensuing melee two passengers and one of the American crew members, William Bernstein, were killed. The British Marines used truncheons and the passengers threw everything they could at the British. Besides the three dead, about twenty people were wounded. The superstructure of the ship had been badly damaged and the 4,500 passengers were distraught. Ruth Gruber was a correspondent on board one of the subsequent ships that the passengers were transferred to and has vividly described the living conditions for the 4,500 passengers jammed aboard a ship designed to carry 400 soldiers. The *Exodus 1947* was eighteen hundred tons. Most cruise ships today are anywhere from 100,000 to 250,000 tons. *Oasis of the Seas*, which carries five thousand passengers and is owned by Royal Caribbean, an Israeli company, has an atrium, rock climbing walls, and seven swimming pools. *Exodus 1947* had the horrible bunks like those found in Auschwitz, with untenable sanitary conditions. What it did have were idealistic people determined to get to what soon would become Israel.

After being intercepted, the ship was towed to Haifa under British command. While the ship was moored in Haifa harbour, Moshe Bitterman described the three ships they were going to be eventually taken to as being prison ships. Thousands of the trapped passengers stood on the decks. Small ships from the Jewish agency were allowed to approach the *Exodus 1947* and attempt to send food aboard. Moshe described biscuits as being filled with worms and a meagre allotment of 1,500 calories per person.

The British government under Clement Atlee and Foreign Minister Aneurin Bevin was in a quandary. Bevin had met the previous winter with a rabbi who was active with the Bricha and who tried to intercede for the Jews. At the meeting Bevin was wearing a scarf and overcoat indoors even while sitting beside a fireplace. Britain was experiencing a particularly cold winter in 1946-1947. Many thought the Jews had sent another plague to torment Britain. It was bitterly cold, with lots of snow and not enough coal, as the country was almost bankrupt. Bevin complained bitterly to the rabbi that the Jews were too pushy a people and that they always wanted to get to the head of the queue. Churchill, who had been voted out of office in 1945, had held a much better attitude towards the Jews. Bevin and Clement Atlee, the prime minister, had no tolerance or sympathy for the Zionist cause and could never understand that they were dealing with Holocaust survivors.

Bevin, after consultation with General Cunningham about the Exodus, the British High Commissioner, said, "Deport the Jews back to France." Previously illegal immigrants had been sent back to Cyprus, which was under British jurisdiction. This time they decided to deport them back to the country of origin, a policy which was then called "refoulment." The British thought that this would discourage any other countries from allowing the illegal immigrants to depart. As the *Exodus 1947* was very unseaworthy after being rammed by the British ships, the 4,500 passengers were transferred onto three ships, the *Runnymede Park*, *Ocean Vigour*, and *Empire Royal*. These were the three ships that Bitterman described as looking like prison ships. The transfer was very difficult as people resisted and tried to escape. It was on all the Warner Pathe newsreels. Huge amounts of negative publicity for the British were created due to the presence of the worldwide press and UNSCOP (United Nations Special Committee on Palestine). Both the media and the United Nations actively condemned the British.

The deportees on the ship *Ocean Vigour* told a correspondent in a nearby boat that they would rather starve to death than land anywhere but the Holy Land. Upon further questioning from the journalist on whether or not they would get off the boat the replies were, "*Nein, nein!*" (No, no!) followed by more singing of the Hatikvah. The courage shown by the Holocaust survivors who were the original passengers of the *Exodus 1947* saga played out as eight hundred additional wretched Jews, also Holocaust survivors, were seized from two additional illegal immigrant ships.

When the 4,500 passengers of the *Exodus 1947* arrived at Marseille, France, on July 19 aboard the three transport ships, they refused to disembark and the French said they would not force the immigrants off the ships. The exiles said clearly that "none but dead men will be landed here." The French, however, had made elaborate preparations to disembark the refugees, including welcoming invitations in Yiddish, French, and Hebrew. The event became a cause célèbre for thousands of French spectators in the little village of Port de Bouc near Marseille. While most of these Holocaust survivors were young, there were a few older people in addition to many children. A large number of pregnant women were carried aboard these floating coffins. How the British Marines dealt with all of these poor bedraggled people who had been through so much is hard to envision.

The British were stymied, so after a great deal of debate they decided to send the passengers to Hamburg, Germany, in the British Occupied Zone of Germany. British diplomats cautioned there would be enormous negative fallout, that sending Jews from the Holocaust back to Germany seemed to be very poor public relations.

Negative publicity surrounding the displaced persons camps in Germany had appeared months before the *Exodus 1947* events. A large newspaper advertisement appeared in the *New York Times* of December 1946 appealing for the repatriation of the million and a half Hebrews remaining in Europe. The ad stated that the Hebrews should be sent to Palestine whether or not the Royal Navy consented. The ad urged that every man, woman, and child be transported out of the horror, where six million of their loved ones had died, and be transported to Palestine with ships and not words. The advertisement featured a picture of a Nazi concentration camp with a caption, "No Merry Christmas in DP Camps." The wording further urged the need for help for a proud and heroic people and for justice in Palestine. At the same time, as this advertisement appeared a picture was shown of a large group of Jewish displaced persons holding a demonstration under the Arch of Titus in Rome.[18]

As the *Ocean Vigour* arrived at Hamburg more than one thousand British troops surrounded the pier. They were armed with machine guns, rifles, tommy guns, tear gas pistols, steel-tipped clubs, and high pressure water hoses. The jetty was lined with cages to hold any recalcitrant deportees. At the same time jazz music was played through loudspeakers lining the pier. Presumably this was to calm the refugees, but many fainted and collapsed. Then numerous ambulances arrived to take the elderly, sick, and injured to the hospital. As the immigrants packed onto the trains, the Red Cross and British army personnel offered coffee and sandwiches. Many of the Jews threw offerings back at the officials. In Palestine a general strike was called. Flags were lowered to half-mast and the day was designated as "Hamburg Day" to protest the deportations to former Nazi work camps. Initially German police were to guard the Jews but these were soon supplanted by British soldiers. The wise comment was made that the Jews had been behind barbed wire before in Germany. The promise was made that this time the outcome would be different.

On August 22, 1947, the British Foreign Office said that British diplomats should deny that the passengers were being sent back to German concentration camps, but in reality the Jews were sent to former concentration camps and they were kept behind barbed wire. In addition, there were armed guards and watchtowers. The passengers were carefully screened for extremists.

When the passengers were taken off the ships there was very strong resistance. Most of the women, children, and the aged went peacefully, but the men resisted. These 4,500 Holocaust survivors wanted to go to the Promised Land and definitely not back to Germany. The British Marines used water hoses and batons to subdue the Jewish resistors. A particular problem was the ship the *Runnymede Park*. The British report said that the Jews on board were led by a "capable and energetic fanatic," a certain Miry Rosman. One hundred military police and 200 soldiers were mobilized to

---

18 The Arch of Titus commemorated the Roman victory over the Jews in AD 70.

disembark the "fanatical" Jews. Thirty-three were injured in the mêlée and 68 were put on trial for unruly behaviour.

A report by one of the British officers described the incident: "The Jew is liable to panic and 800-900 Jews fighting to get up a stairway to escape tear smoke could have produced a deplorable business." He [Lt. Col. Gregson, the officer in charge] added: "It is a very frightening thing to go into the hold full of yelling maniacs when outnumbered six or eight to one." Describing the assault, the officer wrote to his superiors, "After a very short pause, with a lot of yelling and female screams, every available weapon up to a biscuit, tins of food and bulks of timber were hurled at the soldiers. They withstood it admirably and very stoically until the Jews assaulted and in the first rush several soldiers were downed with half a dozen Jews on top kicking and tearing. No other troops could have done it as well and as humanely as these British ones did." He concluded, "It should be borne in mind that the guiding factor in most of the actions of the Jews is to gain the sympathy of the world press."

Dr. Noah Barou from the Jewish Agency who witnessed the incident on board was traumatized: "They went into the operation as if it were a football match . . . and it seemed evident that they had not had it explained to them that they were dealing with people who had suffered a lot and who were resisting in accordance with their convictions." He noted, "People were usually hit in the stomach and this in my opinion explains that many people who did not show any signs of injury were staggering and moving very slowly along the staircase giving the impression that they were half-starved and beaten up . . . When the people walked off the ship, many of them, especially younger people, were shouting to the troops 'Hitler commandos', 'gentleman fascists', 'sadists'." Dr. Barou was "especially impressed" by one young girl who "came to the top of the stairs and shouted to the soldiers, "I am from Dachau." And when they did not react she shouted 'Hitler commandos'."

After the Jewish passengers were removed, a large homemade bomb was found aboard. The camps they were sent to were indeed described by all as concentration camps, surrounded with barbed wire, but there were no German guards. Nevertheless the allegations would not go away. On October 6, 1947, the British Foreign Office sent telegrams to Germany inquiring about the conditions. The deportees in the camps asserted themselves, "Nothing will deter us from Palestine. Which jail we go to is up to you (the British). We did not ask you to reduce our rations; we did not ask you to put us in Poppendorf and Am Stau."[19]

Twenty-seven hundred of the would-be immigrants to Palestine made their way to the US Zone of occupation in Germany. From there the Bricha smuggled them into Palestine. By April 1948, eighteen hundred remained in the two detention camps. While the *Exodus 1947* drama continued, one migrant was killed and ten more were wounded on another refugee ship named *In Spite of It All* trying to reach Palestine. The *Exodus 1947* prisoners continued to demonstrate, tearing down tents in their camp.

A worn-out British nation announced that it would withdraw from Palestine as soon as it was feasible. At the same time partition was approved at the United Nations. The British Mandate Palestine authorities decided to allow some fifteen hundred immigrants without certificates into the country. Graciously they decided that approximately five hundred babies under two would not be counted against the quota.

On Sunday, May 16, 1948, the banner headline of the *Palestine Post* read, "State of Israel is Born." The first independent Jewish state in nineteen centuries was born in Tel Aviv. As the British Mandate over Palestine came to an end at midnight Friday, May 13. A war began as several Arab armies invaded the new Jewish state from the north, south, and east. The Egyptian air force bombed Tel Aviv, but everywhere the Jewish army fought back.

It took President Truman only ten minutes to recognize the Provisional Jewish Government once the British Mandate had ended. Truman took this action despite strong opposition from many senior advisors, including Secretary of State George C. Marshall. The very first act of the new state

---

[19] British internment camps in postwar Germany for the detainees.

was to rescind the immigration restrictions of the Mandate. The British blockade was over.

Britain held the remaining illegal immigrants in camps in Cyprus until January 1949, when His Majesty's Government finally recognized the State of Israel and these poor, tortured people were finally allowed to make *aliyah*. The United States and Soviet Union had recognized the new state in May 1948.

UNSCOP covered the events and were present in Haifa when the *Exodus 1947* was initially offloaded. The ordeals of the ship and passengers caused, for a time, a media sensation and the British suffered huge embarrassment. The American government under Harry Truman was convinced that the British could not handle the situation and pressured the British to relinquish the mandate to the UN. There is no doubt that the saga of the *Exodus 1947* was a defining moment in the history of British Mandate Palestine.

Saturday, May 15, 1948, a large banner headline in the *New York Times* read, "Zionists Proclaim New State of Israel, Truman Recognizes It and Hopes For Peace; Tel Aviv is Bombed, Egypt Orders Invasion." The paper went on to say, "The Jews rejoice. Some Weep as Quest for Statehood Ends." "White Paper Dies." "Help of UN Asked" "New Regime Holds Out Hand to Arabs." "US Gesture Acclaimed."

In 1958 Leon Uris wrote *Exodus* partly based on the events involving Exodus 1947. In 1960, *Exodus* the movie was directed by Otto Preminger, a non-Jew. It stared Paul Newman and Eva Marie Saint as well as Sal Mineo as an Irgun terrorist. In 1997 Morley Safer narrated a documentary *Exodus 1947* on PBS.

The declaration of independence of the State of Israel is still seared in childhood memories. In 1948 children attending the Cheder (Hebrew and religious training) at Shareii Shomayim synagogue on St. Clair Avenue in Toronto were told that the state had come into being. Buses were assembled and we were told to line up and dress in white shirts and dark pants. We were taken by bus to the Brunswick Ave "Y." We had to line up like a choir and sing. We sang Hatikvah and then other Hebrew songs. As I didn't sing well and still don't maybe that's not a part of the memory that resonates. But what is seared into my mind were the Israeli flags and the large picture of Theodore Herzl.

The damaged ship formerly known as the *President Warfield*, renamed *Exodus 1947*, was moored to a breakwater in Haifa Harbour, until it burned to the waterline in 1952. It was sold as scrap iron to an Italian firm in 1963.

The Exodus 1947

The damage to her superstructure by the collision with the British destroyers is clearly visible in this photo taken of EXODUS as she docked at Haifa.

The Exodus, after the ramming by the British.

Crowded conditions below deck

Conditions below deck on the Exodus.

Disembarking refugees from the Exodus to Hamburg, Germany.

Lord Moyne

Harold Macmichael (front center-holding hat)

CONCLUSION

Why did British policy towards the acceptance of Jewish refugees from Nazi occupied Europe into Palestine evolve the way it did? Why was there a blockade of Palestine by both land and sea? Why was there so little acceptance of Jews to fight in the British Armed forces against their common foe the Nazis until almost the end of the war? Why was the *Struma* sent to certain death? Why was the *Exodus 1947*, filled with some five thousand refugees, Holocaust survivors, rammed by two British destroyers? Why were unarmed refugee ships fired upon by British naval vessels? Why was every attempt to liberate Jews from certain death rebuffed with such finality?

The answers are many and complex. Perhaps the first answer is British anti-Semitism. Bernard Wasserstein, in his book *Britain and the Jews of Europe*, quotes AR Dew, head of the Southern department of the British Foreign Office, as saying, "In my opinion a disproportionate amount of this office is wasted in dealing with these wailing Jews." Dew said the above in December 1944 when the facts of the Holocaust were only too well known. A Sir John Shuckburgh, the deputy undersecretary of the Colonial Office, is quoted by Wasserstein as saying, "I am convinced that in their hearts they hate us and have always hated us. They hate all Gentles." A third quote from Wasserstein concerns a JS Bennett of the Colonial office, who said that "the Jews have done nothing but add to our difficulties by propaganda and deeds since the war began." Even after the war, when the full extent of the horrors of the extermination of European Jewry were open for all to see Aneurin Bevan, the British Labour foreign minister, was quoted as saying, "The Jews are always pushing to get to the head of the queue."

The anti-Semitism of wartime Britain fit in with the general mood and paranoia of the time. After the catastrophic defeat of France in May 1940 the hysteria reached a boiling point. German spies were said to be everywhere and there was no question in the public's mind that the Jewish refugees were infiltrated with hordes of Nazis. Yet there was not one single documented case of Nazis disguising themselves as Jews during World War II. Nevertheless, thousands of Jews of German origin who had found their way to the safety of the British Isles were interned and eventually exiled to faraway places like Canada and Australia.

Amongst these unfortunate deportees was a young rabbinical student named Erwin Schild, who later became a prominent rabbi in Toronto, Canada. Schild described his embarkation at Three Rivers, Quebec, as a harrowing experience. A cordon of heavily armed Canadian soldiers surrounded the mostly religious refugees, most of whom were pious Hassidim and of German origin. In addition to the rifles and fixed bayonets, several heavy machine guns mounted on tripods watched over the Jews as sandbags and barbed wire contained the disembarking passengers.

Amongst the group of Canadian soldiers guarding the refugees was a Jewish sergeant. When he reached home in Montreal, the sergeant immediately called the Canadian Jewish Congress to report the events. After a few months conditions improved and the students were provided with books and better food. Most were able to resume their studying and praying.

Another factor that influenced the British blockade was disbelief that the Holocaust was occurring on the part of key officials. When purported German atrocities in World War I were proven to be propaganda the tenuous basis for nonbelief of the Holocaust was founded. By the time Anthony Eden rose in the House of Commons on December 17, 1942, to condemn Nazi attacks on the Jews, it was clear that much was known. It is also known that German radio codes concerning mass shootings of Jews in the invasion of the Soviet Union were deciphered as early as 1941. There is no question that the murder of the Jewish people was an established fact.

Perhaps another aspect of the British blockade was the lack of any connections with the Jews of Europe. The Jews were viewed as stateless people who wandered from place to place. The upper class British civil servants who sat in their comfortable clubs, smoked their cigars, drank their brandy, and made fateful decisions had no connection with these refugees. The British Empire and the dominions that they represented had no room for these pitiful people.

One man towered above this indifference; however, Winston Spencer Churchill had to lead a nation in a struggle for its very survival. All the proposals that Churchill made were mired in a bureaucratic quagmire and few if any surfaced to help the Jews find a refuge.

British foreign policy regarding Jewish immigration to Palestine was focused on appeasing the Arabs and safeguarding their strategic interests. As Rommel and his Panzer units approached Egypt and then perhaps Palestine, the Yishuv reacted. Tens of thousands of Jews volunteered to fight with the British to defend British Palestine. In contrast scant numbers of Arabs volunteered, most of who soon deserted after receiving monetary allowances. Palestinian Arab contributions to the British war effort were the bare minimum. Indeed, Husseini, the Grand Mufti of Jerusalem, spent most of the war years in Hitler's company in Berlin.

Most Arabs in the area strongly supported the German cause, including such future luminaries as Anwar Sadat. As far as strategic concerns, most British officials, excepting a few like Churchill, could never grasp the fact that the Jews could form a state and defend themselves. A more forward looking British administration might have realised that the future Jewish state that they could not conceive of would eventually be a strategic asset to defend British and Western interests.

Perhaps another additional aspect of British policy was British proclivity towards the Arabs. Harkening back towards the romantic and exotic connections of T.E. Lawrence and the Arabs the British foreign office was filled with so-called Arabists whose sympathies lay with the Arabs. Indeed Anthony Eden himself said "that he preferred Arabs to Jews."

The British in Palestine always acted like they were on parade. They were smug and superior with upper-class attitudes honed by years of colonial administration supervising uneducated natives in Africa and India. While there were many Arab elites in Palestine the vast majority were uneducated peasants (fellahin). The British had no trouble dealing with the uneducated, but the vast majority of Jews gave them a lot of trouble. The British simply were not used to supervising people with the zeal and fervour of the Zionists. Almost from the mid-1920s onwards there was constant friction between the Jews and the British.

In contrast, when they dealt with the Arabs they had a sense of mission reinforced by their perception of psychological ascendancy over the Arabs. All this was supported by the very English lives they led in Palestine. As the historian Bernard Wasserstein put it, the British possessed a coherent imperial attitude with rigid social behaviour.

British literature describing the time, even that written years later, had almost no mention of the Holocaust and its effect on the Jews, those in Palestine or even the survivors. It never clicked with the British mindset that the Holocaust survivors needed to be shown some amount of special sympathy. The British were only worried that the Jews might push to the front of the proverbial queue.

Mrs. Meyerson, the future Golda Meir and then political head of the Jewish agency in Palestine, told a British official that the British could not understand "what it felt like to be an independent people and nation after two thousand years of endeavour." The British official Sir Henry Gurney, replied "that this Jewish achievement in Palestine was being built on a foundation of lies, chauvinism, suspicion, and deception." His comments about the Jews of Palestine do not quite dovetail with the British recognition that the Jews built Mandate Palestine into a viable state, a state that the Zionists built under a first-class British administration. Almost all sensible British authorities admitted that the Jews, with their financial support from abroad, their enthusiasm, and their hard work, had built a quasi-state under British rule.

It is also interesting to note that the British had absolutely no hope of any Jewish triumph in Palestine. It was simply inconceivable to the many British officials commenting on the situation that there would be a future Israeli state. How wrong they were.

Paul Johnson, a noted historian, once said that history is one long argument. It is also an underlying series of questions and "what ifs." What if the British had allowed the Jewish people complete access to Mandate Palestine in the years 1933-1948? How many thousands, tens of thousands, even millions would have been saved? If one considers carefully the Intentionalist-Functionalist debate mentioned in the introduction, the ability to emigrate from Germany and then Europe becomes paramount.

It is quite clear despite the debate about Hitler's and Nazi Germany's long-range objectives for the Jews there were many opportunities to escape. Even the Nazis considered refuge for the Jews in places like Madagascar. As Chaim Weizman said, "There was only one place for the Jews, British Mandate Palestine." Great Britain had promised a homeland to the Jewish people in 1917 and in the time of their greatest need blockaded them from their refuge in Palestine. The White Paper of May 1939 virtually stopped Jewish immigration when hundreds of thousands were trying to escape from the impending horrors of Nazi rule. Jews died in Auschwitz and Treblinka while more than 25,000 fought for the allies at El-Alamein and Tobruk in North Africa. At the same time the British blockade turned back refugee ships like the *Struma*, the *Liesel* and the *El Salvador* which all subsequently sank.

The inability of the Jews of Europe to flee to their sole sanctuary cost the Jewish people and the world dearly.

EPILOGUE

The survivors of the fight to break the British blockade found many different ways to resume their lies after the horrors of World War II. Many did stay in Israel, while others went on to settle in Canada and the United Sates. The late 1940s and early 1950s were an intensely difficult time in the new state of Israel, called the Tzena (severe austerity). People did not have proper housing and stayed in what we call trailers and they called caravans. Although there was no starvation, food was bland and monotonous. Even the bare essentials were hard to come by. Yet these people as a group proved extraordinarily resilient.

Miriam Beckerman was one of the few interviewed who came to British Mandate Palestine legally. She lived through a tumultuous time at the start of the Israeli state and eventually returned to, Canada where she found a career as a Yiddish translator. Miriam still maintains a strong connection with Israel.

Moshe Bitterman came to Toronto, Canada, and became a success. He became the Shamus (beadle) of a large conservative synagogue, Beth Tikvah. Moshe successfully tutored a generation of Bar and Bat Mitzvah students, including two of the author's sons. All of these students came away with a strong knowledge of Zionism and Hebrew instilled in them.

Claudia Bloch still has strong roots in Israel and has vivid memories of her father holding her aloft to show the Italians that they were friendly refugees and not enemies. She spent many years in Israel and still supports it strongly. She still retains her childhood memory of drying clothes on the roof of the apartment building in Tel Aviv.

Felicia Carmelli still remembers the Holocaust and speaks at educational meetings about Transnistria in Romania.

Alexander Eisen wrote a book, *Time of Fear*, and had a successful career in electronics. He still has strong connections with Israel after serving with the intelligence services.

Alexander Gomulka spent over three months in Atlit and still remembers the rotten tomatoes.

Shlomo Goldhaber was very successful in the jewellery business in Haifa and still had profound memories of watching the Eichmann trial and breaking down.

Jacob Goldstein came to Canada after contributing to Israel in many ways. He had successful careers in the building business and kitchen furniture.

Moshe Grossinger became a success in the food service industry as well as a pillar in B'nai Brith, a Jewish service organization.

Mickey Kestenbaum had a long and successful career in the clothing business in Toronto and acquired a history degree at the University of Toronto while in his eighties.

Laslo Leung spent many years in Israel after 1948 and served with distinction in the Israeli navy for four years.

Arie Lewin and his wife Gerda both served with the IDF in the War of Independence. Arie was given a special citation and promoted to major.

Henry Melnyk helped open the Burma Road in the War of Independence. He returned to Warsaw in 1993 at the commemoration of the Warsaw ghetto uprising and is still a strong supporter of Israel along with the rest of the interviewees.

After serving in both the Israeli Police forces and Israeli army, Ben Miller immigrated to Canada in 1952. After a succession of different businesses and vocations he launched a successful career with his beloved brother Sol as a developer and entrepreneur.

The three Shene orphans all had successful lives and have lived in Israel, France and Canada. Samuel Shene returned to France in 2010.

Henry Wellisch immigrated to Canada from Israel in 1951, settling in Montreal before moving to Toronto in 1969. He had a long and successful career as a mechanical and architectural designer.Bibliography

BIBLIOGRAPHY

Interviews

Miriam Beckerman
August 19, 2010
Born: Toronto, August 1927

Claudia Bloch
November 3, 2010
Born: February 1938

Felicia Carmelly
July 17, 2010
Born: Romania Sept 25, 1931

Alexander Eisen
November 29, 2010
Born: 1929

Alexandar Gamulka
August 10, 2010
Born: Bucharest, Romania 1939

Shlomo Goldhaber
November 12, 2010
Born: January 1919

Moshe Grossinger
July 31, 2010
Born: Lodz, Poland 1943

Mickey Kistenbaum
December 3, 2010
Born: July 8, 1918

Laslo Leung
August 18, 2010
Born: May 1925

John Mecklenberg
By phone from London, England, September 2010
Born: Sept 2, 1938

Henry Melnyik
January 19, 2010
Born: Lodz, Poland 1922

Samuel Shene
July 6, 2010
Born: Belfort, France March 1936

Henry Wellisch
July 18, 2011
Born: Vienna, Austria, 1922

Secondary Sources

Abba, Eban
Israel through My Eyes
G. P. Putnam
New York 1992

Abba, Eban
My People Story of the Jews
Random House
New York 1968

Begin, Menachem
The Revolt
Steimatzky House
Bnei Brak, Israel 1972

Ben Gurion, David
Memoirs
World Publishing Company
New York 1970

Black, Edwin
The Transfer Agreement
Dialog Press
Washington DC 1984

Collier Basil
A Short History of WWII
Collins Press
London 1967

Devork, Deborah and Robert Jar Van Pelt
Flight from the Reich
Refugee Jews 1933-1946
WW Norton and Company
New York 2009

Frantz, Douglas and Collins Catherille
Death on the Black Sea
Harper Collins
New York 2003

Gilbert, Martin
Churchill and the Jews: A Lifelong Friendship
Henry Holt and Company
New York 2007

Gruber, Ruth
*Destination Palestine: The Story of Haganah Ship
Exodus*
Current Books 1948

Habas, Bracha
The Gate Breakers
Herzl Press
London 1963

Holly, David
Exodus 1947
Little Brown and Co
Toronto 1969

Mallmann, Klaus-Michael and Cuppers, Martin
Nazi Palestine
Enigma Books
New York 2005

Marador, Munya
Haganah
New American Library
New York 1957

Nicosia, Francisce
The Third Reich and the Palestine Question
Transaction Publishers
Rutgers
New Jersey, USA 1944/2000

Patt, Avinoam J.
Funding Home and Homeland
Wayne State University Press
Detroit, Michigan 2009

Porat, Dina
The Blue and Yellow Star of David
Harvard University Press
London 1990

Rubinstein, William D
Myth of Rescue
Routledge
London 1997

Shalim Avi
The Iron Wall
W. W. Norton
New York 2000

Shmuel, Katz
Lone Wolf Part I and Part II
Vladimir Jabotinsky
Barricade Books
New York

Stone, I. F.
Underground to Palestine
Hutchinson of London
London 1978

Teveth Shabtai
Ben Gurion and the Holocaust
Harcourt Brace
New York 1996

Walter, Laquer
A History of Zionism
MJF Books
New York 1972

Wasserstein, Bernard
Britain and the Jews of Europe
Oxford University Press
Oxford England 1988

Yoram, Hazony
The Jewish State
The Struggle For Israel's Soul
Basic Books
New York 2000

Zertal, Idith
Holocaust Survivors and the Emergence of Israel
University of California Press
Berkley, CA 1998

Archival Sources

Jewish Agency for Israel
Central Bureau Settlement
German Jews
Report XXII Congress Basel

Jewish Agency for Palestine
Central Bureau for the Settlement of German Jews
Report to XIX Congress
And Tel Aviv Counsel of the Jewish Agency in Levine
Published July 1935

Jewish Agency for Palestine
Central Bureau for the Settlement of German Jews
Report to XIX Congress
And Tel Aviv Counsel of the Jewish Agency in Levine
Zurich 1937

Royal Institute of International Affairs

Great Britain and Palestine 1915-1936
Information Dept Paper #20

Strauss Memoir
Jewish Immigrants in the Nazi Period
Leo Baeck Archive*   .

GLOSSARY

Clement Attlee 1883-1967
British Prime Minister 1945-1951

Menachem Begin
The successor to Jabotinsky in the then Revisionist movement
Later Prime Minister of Israel 1977

David Ben Gurion 1886-1973
The First Prime Minister of the State of Israel and the

Neville Chamberlain 1869-1940
British Prime Minister 1937-1940

Winston Leonard Churchill 1874-1965
British Prime Minister 1940-1945 **el-Husseini Haj Amin** 1895-1974
A political and religious leader of the Palestinian Arabs

Ben Hecht 1893-1964
An author, playwright, and journalist who worked with Hillel Kook to organize illegal Jewish Immigration to Palestine

Theodore Herzl 1860-1904
The spark who ignited Modern Zionism

Hillel Kook (Peter Bergson)
Established the committee for a Jewish Army and the emergency committee for the Rescue of European Jews

Sir Harold MacMichael 1882-1969
High Commissioner for Palestine and Transjordan 1938-1944

Malcolm McDonald 1901-
Secretary State for the Colonies 1938-1940

Lord Moyne 1880-1944
Deputy Minister of State Middle East
1942-1943, assassinated November 1944

Herbert Samuel 1870-1963
First High Commissioner to Palestine 1920-1925, who was also Jewish

Hanna Senesch
A poet and Jewish heroine who parachuted into Nazi occupied Europe to warn Hungarian Jews of the Holocaust

Henrietta Szold 1860-1945
Founder of Hadassah and mother of youth immigration

Chaim Weizmann 1874-1952
Helped initiate the Balfour Declaration and first President of Israel 1949-1952

Vladamir Zeev Jabotinsky 1880-1940
The charismatic initial leader of the Revisionist Zionist Movement

Terms

Aliyah: Ascent Jewish immigration to the Land of Israel

Bricha: Flight the movement to lead Holocaust survivors out of Europe to Palestine

Chalutz: Pioneers Agricultural Labourers in Palestine

Chanich: Student or trainee, a term used to refer to members of Zionist youth groups

Displaced Persons (DPs): Displaced refugees

Eretz Israel: Land of Israel

Ha'apalah: Upward struggle, clandestine immigration to Palestine

Hachsharah: Preparation, agricultural and other training in preparation for Aliyah in a collective setting

Kibbutz: agricultural settlements in Palestine and the Diaspora where they prepared Olim for Jewish immigration to Palestine

Madrich: Leader of a Zionist youth group

Olim: Jewish immigrants to Palestine

ORT (Organizational Rehabilitation and Training): a Jewish organization that helped many.

Shaliach: An emissary, a representative from the Yishuv assigned to promote immigration from the Diaspora

She'erit Hapletah: The surviving remnant the term used to refer to the community of Jewish Holocaust survivors in Europe

Yishuv: Settlement to the Jewish community in British Mandate Palestine until its end in May 1948

Zionist Youth Groups

Betar: Right-wing revisionist youth movement

Dror: Socialist pioneering youth movement founded in Poland

Gordoniah: Socialist non-Marxist youth movement from Poland named after A. D. Gordon

Hashomer Hatzair: Extreme left wing Zionist youth movement from Marxist ideology

Hehalutz: Pioneer movement and umbrella organization of Zionist youth that trained members for *aliyah* to Palestine

Lehi: Fighters for freedom in Israel, an offshoot of the Stern gang after A. Stern was killed by the British most radical group

Haganah: Paramilitary organization formed by the left wing Zionists in British Mandate Palestine which existed from 1920 to 1948, eventually evolved into the Israeli Armed Forces

Irgun: The National Military organization of the Revisionist party in Israel which broke from the mainstream Haganah in 1931.

Mapai: Left-wing Zionist party which became the Israeli Labour Party

Palmach: Elite force of the Haganah

Revisionists: Israeli right wing political party initially led by Vladimir Zeev Jabotinsky and later by Menachem Begin; the party underwent several name changes as it became the Herut Party, then the Likud Party and eventually the basis for the present day Kadima Party

www.ingramcontent.com/pod-product-compliance
Lightning Source LLC
Chambersburg PA
CBHW021559280526
45784CB00001BA/417